NORWELL

David Ken.

0131 - 447 -
3814

HOME
FROM HOME

THIRD EDITION

THE COMPLETE GUIDE TO HOMESTAYS & EXCHANGES

CENTRAL ⬡ BUREAU
FOR EDUCATIONAL VISITS & EXCHANGES

LONDON   EDINBURGH   BELFAST

Third edition October 1994
© Central Bureau for Educational Visits & Exchanges

ISBN 0 900087 99 4

Published by the Central Bureau for
Educational Visits & Exchanges, Seymour Mews,
London W1H 9PE
℄ 0171-725 9402   fax 0171-935 5741
Editorial Director Tony Male
Head of Publications Thom Sewell
Editor Moira Jenkins

Cover illustration: Thomas Lochray/Image Bank

A Year Between was compiled, edited and
produced for print by the Information, Print
& Design Unit, Central Bureau for Educational
Visits & Exchanges, London

Printed and bound in Britain by Page Bros, Norwich

USING THIS GUIDE

The opportunities in *Home from Home* are detailed under separate sections covering HOMESTAYS, EXCHANGES, TERM STAYS and HOME EXCHANGES. Organisations offering opportunities are listed alphabetically within these sections. Two further sections, PRACTICAL INFORMATION and COUNTRY PROFILES offer complementary advice to make *Home from Home* a comprehensive guide to the whole field of international homestays and exchanges.

Homestays The homestay information is provided under three subsections covering mainland Europe, the British Isles and other countries worldwide. A homestay involves being welcomed into a home in another country and being treated as a member of the family and in a wider context, of the local community. Children and young adults are usually placed in a home where there is someone of a similar age. You will learn about the family's attitudes and values by taking part in their day-to-day routine and activities and consequently improve your ability and vocabulary in the host language.
At the outset a homestay is strictly one-way; in practice participants often find that their compatibility with their hosts is such that the homestay develops into an exchange, the partner visiting them in their own home at some later stage.

Exchanges The exchanges information is in two subsections, covering exchanges within Europe, and beyond. An exchange operates on much the same basis as a homestay, the difference being that hospitality is reciprocated when the exchange partner is welcomed into your own home. This may take place consecutively, your partner accompanying you on your journey home, or will happen in the next holiday period or even the following year. The matching procedure is particularly important if the exchange is to be successful, and every care should be taken to ensure that you provide an accurate picture of yourself, your interests and your community environment.

Term stays A term stay involves attending a foreign school for one or two terms, or for a full academic year, and can operate either on a homestay or exchange basis. Participants become totally immersed not just in family life, but in school and community life as well. If a term stay is planned in a country whose language is not your own, an adequate command of the language will be necessary to cope not only with everyday life but also with classroom learning. In addition, the curriculum may be radically different from your own, and allowance must be made for adaptation and for catching up on your return.

Home exchanges The idea of exchanging homes, either for a holiday or for longer periods, is becoming increasingly popular as the concept of responsible tourism spreads. This section provides information on agencies who offer an exchange service, usually through listings directories.

Key to symbols and entry format

Information has been provided in a set format as detailed below:

 Name and address of organisation

 Telephone and fax numbers Where no number is given, written enquiries are preferred. The UK area codes given in this guide reflect the recent changes made: eg London 071 has become 0171. Five major cities, Bristol, Leeds, Leicester, Nottingham and Sheffield, have a new area code and local numbers increase from six to seven digits, gaining an extra 9 or 2. The international access code from the UK has changed from 010 to 00.

Profile Each agency or organisation listed is of a bona fide status. A general description of the aims and activities of each organisation is given here, together with its date of foundation, status (whether commercial, private, non-profitmaking or charitable) and main fields of activity.

Name and address of agents in other countries where direct applications can be made.

Countries/areas and length of stay Some organisations specialise in certain cities or regions, others can place participants throughout the host country. Most are able to arrange stays in a variety of areas, both urban and rural. As much information as possible has been provided, but it is always worth checking with the organisation if you have a preference for an area which is not specifically mentioned. However, you should remember that the first priority for a successful homestay or exchange is identifying a suitable host family. Particularly in the case of an exchange, insisting on a specific area will reduce the number of potential host families and extend the matching period. The average homestay or exchange generally lasts 2-3 weeks, but many organisations are able to arrange shorter or longer stays according to individual requirements. Term stays can last from one term to a full academic year.

Matching By far the most important factor on a homestay, and particularly with an exchange, is to have the most compatible host family. Entries give details of the matching procedure, and most of the organisations listed here place strong emphasis on this, particularly in the case of young people. Whilst a few organisations do try to meet participants personally, the majority depend entirely on the information provided on the application form to make a match. Applicants should therefore take considerable care and effort in completing the application form and give the fullest details of their interests and background. The exchange organisation may take up to three months to find a partner that will make a successful exchange, and applications should always be made as early as possible. The more notice you are able to give an organisation, particularly for exchanges, the better your chance of achieving a good match, not only in terms of host family, but in country, area and dates.

Who is catered for Some organisations deal mainly with individuals, others can cater for groups or families.

Age range Generally speaking, homestays are open to ages 8-80, although the majority of placements are made in the 14-21 age range, where students approaching GCSEs, A levels or other exams can most benefit from being immersed in a foreign language or culture.

Language requirements and tuition Many organisations prefer participants to have at least a basic knowledge of the language of the country they plan to visit. If you have no or limited knowledge of the language, you should, if you are to get the most out of your stay, and as a matter of courtesy, try and learn at least a little of the everyday vocabulary. Many organisations can arrange language courses during the period of the homestay or exchange.

Activities Most host families will be only too happy to include the visitor in their activities and to make a special effort to arrange visits and excursions. Many organisations can arrange additional leisure and sport activities during the stay, and these are often included in the cost of the visit.

Accommodation This is usually arranged in single bedrooms, except where young people may wish to share. Most organisations will place only one visitor with a particular family at a time, ensuring that guests get the best opportunity to practise the host language. Where this is not the case, the organisation will not normally place guests of the same nationality, to ensure that the visitors will not opt for talking in their native language, but instead genuinely communicate in the host language. Some stays offer the options of half board or bed and breakfast, but the majority of stays, particularly those for younger age groups, include full board. Any special dietary needs should be stated on the application form.

Costs Wherever possible, the full cost of the stay or programme has been given. Unless otherwise indicated, costs quoted generally include the fee paid to the agency to cover administrative costs, and meals, accommodation and often travel and insurance. Costs will vary depending on the area, the facilities the host family is able to offer, and the type of board provided. Where additional costs are involved, for example insurance, excursions, escorted travel or tuition fees, these are indicated. Where costs have been given other than in £ Sterling, exchange rates at the time of publication have been given in the COUNTRY PROFILES section.

Travel Many organisations either include travel in the cost of the stay or are able to offer assistance with making arrangements. Often organised travel is in escorted groups, particularly useful for young people not used to travelling alone. Host families will often meet their guests at the port, airport or railway station of arrival. If you are making your own arrangements you should contact the host family to arrange details and check whether they will be able to help with travel to the departure point for the return journey. Further advice is given under PRACTICAL INFORMATION.

Insurance Insurance cover is not always included in the price of the stay, but is often available at extra cost. Even if insurance is included, check that the policy covers all your requirements and not just third party liability. See the PRACTICAL INFORMATION section for further details.

Other services Details of the organisation's related services and activities are included here, for example penfriend services and other visits and language opportunities, and if these are of interest you should write for further information.

Handicapped participants Certain organisations are able to arrange stays for handicapped people, and these are indicated by the initial **H** at the end of the entry. When applying, state the exact nature of the disability and any special care or facilities required.

FIYTO indicates a member of the Federation of International Youth Travel Organisations, which aims to promote educational, cultural and social travel among young people.

FIOCES indicates a member of the Fédération Internationale des Organisations de Correspondances et d'Échanges Scolaires, founded in 1929 to help bring together young people by furthering international school exchanges. Member organisations must provide sufficient moral, pedagogical and technical guarantees.

SAGTA indicates a member of the School & Group Travel Association.

UNOSEL indicates a member of the Union National des Organisations de Séjours Linguistiques.

ABTA indicates a member of the Association of British Travel Agents.

The PRACTICAL INFORMATION section provides advice and information for those intending to take part in a homestay, exchange or term stay, as well as guidelines for host families. It includes suggestions on preparation, what to take with you, insurance, travel and dealing with any problems.

COUNTRY PROFILES lists all the countries covered by *Home from Home*, giving details of embassies, tourist offices, youth and student information centres and suitable travel companies. It also details entry regulations and lists useful publications and other sources of information. In addition, details of opportunities for short-term homestays in the form of bed and breakfast accommodation, and for farm holidays are also given.

APPLICATIONS Once you have decided on the type of visit and have been in touch with a suitable organisation, you should read their literature and application forms very thoroughly. Make sure that you know exactly what is covered by the basic fee; for example, the insurance cover, if any, provided, what the travel arrangements are and what provisions are made for illness or accidents, or for returning home if serious difficulties should arise. If there are any points which are unclear, or if you have any other queries, you should contact the organisation to receive clarification. Whatever type of stay you choose, you should ideally allow a period of 2-3 months so that all the necessary arrangements can be made. Requests for further information and applications themselves should be addressed to the organisations direct, and not to the Central Bureau.

HOMESTAYS

MAINLAND
EUROPE

FRANCE

Accueil France Famille   5 rue François Coppée, 75015 Paris, France

(33 1) 45 54 22 39   Fax (33 1) 45 58 43 25

A non-profitmaking organisation founded in 1985 with the aims of strengthening the ties of friendship and understanding between France and other countries

Homestays arranged in Paris and throughout the French provinces. 1+ weeks, all year. To help with selecting a family, applicants submit details of their hobbies, studies and interests.

Individuals, groups and couples

Ages 16+ (18+ in Paris)

Knowledge of French not necessary, but basic knowledge an advantage. Language tuition for groups on request.

Families help visitors discover the region they are staying in

Bed & breakfast/half/full board accommodation in carefully selected families; single bedrooms. Only one foreign visitor in the family at any one time.

Cost from FF1,350 bed & breakfast per week. FF285 registration fee.

Participants are given relevant information to help in arranging travel. In country areas the host family meet guests at station.

Insurance provided

UNOSEL

FRANCE

ACTE International   39 Rue du Sahel, 75012 Paris, France

(33 1) 43 42 48 84   Fax (33 1) 43 41 51 17

A non-profitmaking organisation founded in 1976 promoting, in collaboration with the French education authorities, educational and cultural travel for students and young people

Homestays arranged in the Paris area. 2/3 weeks, all year.

Individuals and groups

Ages 18+

Basic knowledge of French required. Homestays with French language programmes organised in Brittany during July.

Host families organise visits to local places of interest

Half board, single room accommodation in family home

Cost from FF3,100, 2 weeks; FF4,450, 3 weeks

Participants organise their own travel; coach transfers can be arranged

Insurance not provided

Also arrange study and discovery tours, tailored programmes, French language summer courses and university year programmes

FIYTO

ITALY

Anglo-Italian Holidays 44 Kyrle Road, London SW11 6BA

0171-978 4926

A private organisation set up in 1985 to help young Italians and Britons visit each other's country and sample each other's way of life

Homestays arranged in Tuscany and the areas around Genoa, Venice and Milan. Also, depending on availability, Calabria, Sicily and other areas.

Individuals and adults

Ages 17+

No previous knowledge of Italian necessary. Language courses can be arranged.

No special activities arranged

Student lives as a member of an Italian family, and offers English conversation in return for board and lodging

If very little conversation practice is needed a rent (approx £50-£60 per week) may be required towards living expenses. Registration fee £90.

Participants make own travel arrangements but are normally met on arrival by host family

Insurance not provided

Also arrange au pair stays in England and Italy

FRANCE

Animations Loisirs Jeunes   58 bis, rue Sala, 69002 Lyon, France

(33) 72 40 96 42   Fax (33) 78 37 57 56

A non-profitmaking organisation set up in 1971, arranging activity holidays, linguistic stays, total immersion homestays and exchanges

Homestays arranged in Lyon and surrounding region. 1+ weeks, all year.

Individuals, groups and adults

Ages 9+

Basic knowledge of French required. Language tuition can be arranged.

Excursions organised on request. Host families are also expected to give their guest an idea of French culture, language and people.

Single/shared room in family home

Cost from FF1,205 per week half board and FF1,315 per week full board (students); or FF1,340 per week full board (professionals)

Transfer from Lyon airport can be arranged, cost FF200

Insurance not provided

Also arrange linguistic stays for French children in Germany, Spain, United States and Canada; activity holidays

FRANCE

Aquitaine Service Linguistique 6 Rue Pasteur, 33127 Martignas, France

(33) 56 21 40 96   Fax (33) 56 78 04 01

A non-profitmaking organisation founded in 1978 arranging homestays and language courses

Homestays arranged in the Bordeaux, Cognac, Pays Basque, Perigord and Charentes areas. 1+ weeks, all year.

Individuals, groups, families and adults

Ages 12+

All levels of French accepted. French courses available in Bordeaux and Cognac areas.

Families arrange outings; cultural/sports facilities available in most areas

Single/shared bedrooms in carefully selected families of similar backgrounds and interests, with children of same age where appropriate

Cost FF1,490 full board per week

Participants are normally met at the airport/station by the family

Insurance not provided

Also arrange language courses, exchanges between France/United States

CZECH / SLOVAK REPUBLICS

ARES Martin Gres, PO Box 11, Druzstevnická 20, 736 01 Havírov, Czech Republic

Fax (42 69) 432364

Established in 1991, ARES is a private agency aiming to arrange educational homestays

Homestays arranged mainly in the Czech Republic but also in Slovakia. 2 days-8 weeks, all year.

Individuals and small groups

Ages 10+. Students and teachers welcome.

Knowledge of Czech or Slovak not necessary. Hosts are interested in improving their knowledge of English, French, German, Italian and other languages. Czech language course available.

Hosts are willing to act as tour guides and companions; otherwise no formal activities are organised

Accommodation is in flats, houses or weekend homes with hosts, who are mainly students or teachers. Meals provided by arrangement, usually at a cost of £3/US$4 per day.

Cost from £5/US$7 per person per day, as agreed with hosts, to pay for accommodation. Service charge £20/US$30.

Route maps and timetables provided, and guests are met on arrival at bus or railway stations

Insurance not provided

Also arrange language and activity camps; house rental; Czech language courses

FRANCE

Belaf Study Holidays Banner Lodge, Cherhill, Calne, Wiltshire SN11 8XR

Calne (01249) 812551 Fax (01249) 821533

A professional organisation set up in 1975 by language teachers, and specialising in total immersion homestays for children and adults. Registered in France with the Ministère de Jeunesse et de Sports.

Homestays arranged in Brittany, Normandy, Paris and Nice. 2/3 weeks, all year.

Individuals and groups

Ages 11-18

Basic knowledge of French required. Language work pack can be provided.

Sport and leisure activities, and at least one outing per week organised by the host family

Full board accommodation in carefully selected families

Cost from £200 for 2 weeks plus £30 administration fee.
Homestays can also be conducted on an exchange hospitality basis.

Escorted travel arranged in July and August only. Children are met by host family at point of arrival.

Insurance not provided

H

FRANCE

Club des 4 Vents 104 rue de Vaugirard, 75006 Paris, France

(33 1) 44 39 32 21   Fax (33 1) 45 44 91 56

A non-profitmaking organisation founded in 1947, specialising in international meetings and activities for young people wishing to improve their knowledge of a foreign language and discover other ways of life

Summer homestays with language classes arranged in Arcachon, La Ciotat, Dinan, Montpellier and Sète; 2, 3 or 4 weeks. Year round immersion homestays arranged in Amiens, Arcachon, La Ciotat/St Cyr, Lyon, Montpellier and Paris/Ile de France; 1-4 weeks. Also farmstays in the Perigord region; 3 weeks all year.

Individuals and groups

Ages 12-25, depending on area

One year's knowledge of French required for homestays with language programmes (10-15 hours of classes per week). Two years' knowledge of French for immersion homestays.

Sports activities and excursions included with summer homestays

Full board accommodation with host family. Families are carefully chosen by local coordinators for their warmth and hospitality.

Summer language homestays from FF4,350 - FF6,980 depending on length of stay, activities and area; immersion homestays from FF1,500 for 1 week. Farmstays from FF3,680 for a 3 week session.

Host families meet students at stations/airports

Accident and liability insurance provided

Also arrange residential summer language programmes; French school in Paris offering courses at all levels, all year round

FIYTO

GERMANY

DID Deutsch Institut, Deutsch in Deutschland gmbh
Hauptstraße 26, 63811 Stockstadt/Main, Germany

(49 6027) 41770   Fax (49 6027) 417741

A privately-owned educational organisation founded in 1980, arranging a wide variety of Germany language courses, homestays and academic year programmes

Homestays are arranged throughout Germany in smaller towns and villages. 2+ weeks, all year (places are limited during July and August).

Individuals only

Ages 12-17

Minimum 1 year's knowledge of German required; individual/shared tuition available

Full board accommodation in family home. All families are very carefully selected.

Cost from DM840 for 2 weeks, homestay only; from DM1,545 for 2 weeks including individual tuition

Transfers can be arranged from nearest airport to centre; supplement payable

Accident and illness insurance arranged; supplement payable

FIYTO

FRANCE

Dragons International The Old Vicarage, South Newington, Banbury, Oxfordshire OX15 4JN

Banbury (01295) 721717 Fax (01295) 721991

A commercial organisation founded in 1975 and specialising in individual exchanges and homestays

Homestays arranged throughout France. 2 weeks, March-August.

Individuals only

Ages 11-19

Basic knowledge of French required

Host families arrange outings

Full board accommodation; single/shared rooms in carefully selected families having young people of similar age or background

Cost £169-£199 depending on point of departure from Britain. Costs cover return travel, administrative costs and insurance. Additional charge of £20 per day, board and accommodation.

Fully supervised coach transport from 17 points in Britain to 11 points in France

Fully comprehensive insurance provided

UNOSEL

FRANCE

Échanges Culturels Internationaux 62 avenue Delattre de Tassigny, 13100 Aix-en-Provence, France

(33) 42 21 07 68

A non-profitmaking organisation founded in 1975, arranging homestays with French families

Homestays arranged in Provence and on the Côte d'Azur. 1-4 weeks, all year.

Individuals and groups

Ages 14-30

At least 2 years' study of French required. Language tuition arranged for groups on request.

Families arrange outings. Excursions can be arranged for groups.

Half or full board accommodation in family home. Families are chosen with great care by local organisers; where possible hosts will have children of the same age.

Cost FF1,400 per week full board

Guests are met at railway stations and transferred to host family; extra charge for airport transfers

Public liability insurance provided

Also offer tailor-made tours for groups

FRANCE, GERMANY, ITALY, SPAIN

En Famille Overseas The Old Stables, 60B Maltravers Street, Arundel, Sussex BN18 9BG

Arundel (01903) 883266

A private company founded in 1945 offering holidays for travellers wishing to learn or practise a foreign language in private family homes abroad

Homestays arranged throughout France, Germany, Italy and Spain. 1+ weeks all year.

Individuals, groups, families and adults

Ages 12+

About 2 years' study of the respective language required. French courses can be arranged in Paris, La Rochelle and Tours; optional teaching facilities for school groups.

Guests take part in family outings

Host families are all personally inspected. Particular care is taken to match the family with the individual's requirements, details of background, interest and facilities being carefully compared. Participants must provide two references. The choice of areas/families will be more limited outside France.

Cost £145-£200 half board, £167-£225 full board, per week. Registration fee £20, selection and booking fee £20.

Host families can meet visitors at airport/station at extra cost

Insurance provided

Also arrange teenage group holidays and language courses in France

FRANCE, GERMANY, SPAIN

Euro-Academy Ltd 77a George Street, Croydon, Surrey CR0 1LD

0181-686 2363   Fax 0181-681 8850

A private organisation founded in 1971 to develop the relationships between young people by bringing them together on both study and activity courses

Homestays arranged in France (Amiens, Annecy, Arcachon, Caen, Montpellier, Nice, Paris, Sète, Tours), Germany (Aschaffenburg, Berlin, Hamburg, Mainz, Munich, Wiesbaden) and Spain (Madrid, Malaga, Nerja, Salamanca, Valencia, Zamora). 2/3 weeks, all year.

Individuals and groups

Ages 12-26

Minimum 2 years' language study recommended. Language courses can be combined with family stays.

Sports options (tennis, windsurfing, riding) available on vacation courses

Full board accommodation in families selected for their hospitality. Usually twin bedrooms; single room on request.

France: £220 per week; Germany: £205 per week; Spain: £145 per week (basic homestay). France: £499 per week; Germany £305 per week; Spain £330 per week (combined with language tuition).

Travel arranged. Transfers from airport/station of arrival on request.

Package travel insurance provided

Also offer all year farm stays in south west France; academic year in France and Germany; language study tours for school groups

ABTA FIYTO SAGTA

GERMANY

Europa-Sprachclub GmbH Diezstraße 4A, 70565 Stuttgart, Germany

(49 711) 74 10 61 Fax (49 711) 74 20 73

A commercial organisation founded in 1959 offering a wide range of linguistic holidays for young people and adults

Homestays arranged in Düsseldorf, Stuttgart, Freiburg, the Black Forest and near Lake Constance. 2+ weeks, all year.

Individuals, groups, families and adults

Ages 15+

One year's knowledge of German required. German courses can be combined with homestays in Düsseldorf and Stuttgart.

Excursions and activity programmes may be arranged, and are included in language course programmes

Full board, single/twin accommodation in family home. Families are individually visited and evaluated.

Cost DM1,000, 2 weeks; DM480 for each additional week; DM2,920, 6 weeks; DM3,880, 8 weeks. Extra charge of DM60 for homestays over the Christmas period.

Participants can be met by host family

Third party liability insurance provided

Also offer variety of holiday and intensive, language courses

BELGIUM, DENMARK, FRANCE, GERMANY, ITALY, NETHERLANDS, NORWAY, POLAND, RUSSIA, SPAIN

European Educational Opportunities Programme 28 Canterbury Road, Lydden, Dover, Kent CT15 7ER

Dover (01304) 830948/823631   Fax (01304) 831914/825869

A non-profitmaking organisation founded in 1986 aiming to offer high-quality programmes through carefully selected homes, schools and allied agencies

Homestays arranged in Belgium (Brussels, Antwerp), throughout France and Germany, in Italy (Florence, Rome, Naples, Venice), the Netherlands (Amsterdam, Breda, The Hague) and Spain (Madrid, Valladolid, Salamanca), and possibly in Denmark, Norway, Poland and Russia. 2+ weeks all year.

Individuals, groups, families and adults

Ages 15+

Basic knowledge of the relevant language desirable. Language courses can be arranged.

Excursions arranged

Full board accommodation in family home. Students are totally integrated into the family.

Cost from £196 per week

Participants are met at port of arrival

Insurance not provided

H

AUSTRIA, BELGIUM, FRANCE, GERMANY, GREECE, ITALY, NETHERLANDS, PORTUGAL, SPAIN, TURKEY

Euroyouth Abroad Ltd 301 Westborough Road, Westcliff-on-Sea, Essex SS0 9PT

Southend-on-Sea (01702) 341434   Fax (01702) 330104

A commercial organisation founded in 1961 with the aim of offering facilities for young people to practise the language which they are learning in a family setting and to experience the way of life of the country they are visiting

Homestays arranged in Austria (Vienna and various towns in the provinces), Belgium (French, Dutch or German speaking families in various areas), France (Paris, Aix-en-Provence, Antibes, Cannes, Clermont-Ferrand, Les Sables d'Olonne, Menton, Nice, Tours and small villages along the Côte d'Azur), throughout Germany, Greece (Athens), Italy (Florence, Naples, Perugia), throughout the Netherlands, Portugal (Lisbon), throughout Spain, and in Turkey (Istanbul, Ankara). 2+ weeks, all year. Apply 4-6 weeks in advance (2 months for groups).

Individuals, groups, families and adults

Ages 17+

Basic knowledge of the appropriate language useful. Language courses are available, compulsory in some areas.

Sports activities available; family outings at extra cost

Bed & breakfast, half or full board accommodation in selected and inspected private homes. Welfare service available, advice and assistance provided during stay if required.

Cost £130-£210 per week, depending on country and terms. Registration and placement fee £55.

Insurance not provided but guests must have personal liability cover

Also offer study/sports courses, educational seminars

H   FIYTO   FIOCES

AUSTRIA, BELGIUM, FRANCE, GERMANY, GREECE, ITALY, PORTUGAL, SPAIN, TURKEY

Euroyouth Abroad Ltd (Holiday Guest Stays) 301 Westborough Road, Westcliff-on-Sea, Essex SS0 9PT

Southend-on-Sea (01702) 341434   Fax (01702) 330104

A commercial organisation founded in 1961 with the aim of offering facilities for young people to live in a family setting and experience the way of life of the country they are visiting

Stays arranged throughout Austria, Greece, Italy, Portugal, Spain and Turkey; limited opportunities in Belgium, France and Germany. 2/3 weeks all year. Applicants' mother tongue must be English; early application essential.

Individuals only

Ages 15-25

Basic knowledge of relevant language useful. Language courses available, and are compulsory in some areas.

Opportunities for visits, cultural activities and sports

Full board accommodation with a family provided in return for 3-4 hours daily English conversation with the children or hosts. Time for the guest to practise the host language. Welfare service available; advice and assistance provided during stay if required. Single/twin bedrooms.

Registration fee £10, placement fee £60

Participants arrange their own travel

Insurance not provided but guests must have personal liability cover

Also offer study/sports courses, educational seminars

H FIYTO FIOCES

BELGIUM, CZECH REPUBLIC, DENMARK, FINLAND, FRANCE, GERMANY, HUNGARY, ITALY, NETHERLANDS, POLAND, PORTUGAL, RUSSIA, SLOVAK REPUBLIC, SPAIN, SWEDEN, SWITZERLAND, TURKEY

The Experiment in International Living Otesaga, West Malvern Road, Malvern, Worcestershire WR14 4EN

Malvern (01684) 562577

A non-profitmaking educational travel organisation founded in 1936 with the aim of promoting understanding, friendship and respect between people from different cultural backgrounds. Represented in over 40 countries worldwide; details from UK office.

Homestays arranged throughout Europe. 1-4 weeks, all year.

Individuals, groups and families, adults

Ages 16+

Knowledge of the language not necessary. Courses can be arranged.

Families usually arrange outings. Activities and excursions included in group programmes. Professional courses arranged on request.

Full board accommodation in family home; usually single room, depending on family. Families are carefully selected with the understanding that the aim is to allow individuals to experience a different way of life; the circumstances and beliefs of the host family may therefore differ from those of the participants.

Costs vary depending on country; usually £200-£400, travel extra. Apply 8-10 weeks in advance. Scholarships available.

Group travel arrangements can be made; arrangements for individuals on request. Host families can meet participants at airport/station.

Insurance can be arranged

Also offer special interest programmes, UK/US high school programmes and university placements

SPAIN

Gala Internacional Woodcote House, 8 Leigh Lane, Farnham, Surrey GU9 8HP

Farnham (01252) 715319 Fax (01252) 715319

A private organisation set up in 1981 to organise language and cultural stays in Spain

Gala Internacional, Plaza Narciso Oller 8, 3° 2ª, 08006 Barcelona, Spain (34 3) 415 0850 Fax (34 3) 218 3711

Homestays arranged in Barcelona, on the coast north of Barcelona and in Madrid. 1+ weeks, all year.

Individuals, groups, families and adults

Ages 13-40

At least elementary level of Spanish required. Language tuition available, either 1:1 or in groups.

Sports, activities and excursions organised on request at extra cost. Families will normally arrange outings.

Full board, single room accommodation in family home

Cost Pts32,010 per week (6 nights)

Guests are collected from railway station at no extra cost; transfer from airport to host family can be arranged, cost Pts3,500-Pts4,400 depending on destination

Insurance not provided

FRANCE, GERMANY, SWITZERLAND

GIJK Lingua International Ubierstraße 94, 53173 Bonn, Germany

(49 228) 957300   Fax (49 228) 9573040

A limited company founded in 1983, arranging a variety of international opportunities for young people

Homestays arranged in France (Paris suburbs, Cognac, Lyon, Dourdan, Aix-en-Provence, Dinan, La Ciotat, Montpellier, Sète, Tours, Cannes, Antibes, St Cyr, La Rochelle), Germany (Cologne, Weimar) and Switzerland (Lausanne). 1+ weeks, all year.

Individuals and groups

Ages 12+, depending on area chosen

Some knowledge of French/German desirable. Depending on the area, language and culture courses are included in the homestay programme.

Afternoon cultural excursions, sports and social activities arranged

Full board accommodation (including packed lunch) in family home. Maximum two students of different nationality in each family. All families are visited and carefully selected.

Costs vary depending on area chosen

Help and advice can be given with travel arrangements

Insurance can be provided

Also arrange summer schools and courses; au pair stays worldwide

FRANCE, GERMANY, HUNGARY, ITALY, MALTA, NETHERLANDS, RUSSIA, SPAIN, SWEDEN, UKRAINE

Home Language International Reservations Office, 17 Royal Crescent, Ramsgate, Kent CT11 9PE

Thanet (01843) 851116   Fax (01843) 590300

A commercial organisation set up in 1989 organising immersion language courses where students live with, and are taught by their own teacher

Participants can study French (Paris, Côte d'Azur, Provence, Loire Valley, Bordeaux, Normandy, Brittany), German (Berlin, Frankfurt, Westphalia, Black Forest), Hungarian (Budapest), Italian (Asti, Milan, Tuscany/ Florence), English (Malta), Dutch (Amsterdam), Russian (Moscow, St Petersburg, Black Sea), Spanish (Madrid, Barcelona, Valencia, Salamanca, Andalucia, Canary Islands) and Swedish (Sweden). 1+ weeks, all year. Apply 1 month in advance (2 months for eastern Europe).

Individuals, adults and children

Ages 8+

No previous knowledge of language necessary. Usually 15, 20 or 25 hours language tuition per week.

Excursions and other activities can be provided, if the student wishes, but usually at extra cost where, for example, entrance fees are involved

Full board accommodation in teacher's family home. Shared programme available where two students wish to learn together. Every effort made to match teacher's interests with those of the student. Local organisers visit potential teachers to verify that home is suitable and qualifications genuine, and will also contact students to monitor progress.

Costs according to location and tuition. For example, 1 week in France from FF4,320 (15 hours tuition, shared) to FF7,200 (25 hours, 1:1).

Transfers can be arranged to and from teacher's home at extra cost

Insurance not provided

Also offer business and specialised vocabulary courses, and 5 star luxury specialised courses on the same basis

H

FRANCE, GERMANY, ITALY, SPAIN

Host & Guest Service Harwood House, 27 Effie Road, London SW6 1EN

0171-731 5340   Fax 0171-736 7230

A private organisation founded in 1956, providing a wide variety of reliable accommodation with families according to individual needs

Homestays arranged in France (most areas, especially Brittany, Normandy, Tours and Paris), Germany (Munich), Italy (Florence) and Spain (Barcelona). Length of stay to suit individual requirements.

Individuals, groups and families

All ages; young children will need to be accompanied by an adult

All language levels catered for. Details of local language schools provided on request.

Families may arrange outings

Offer an individual accommodation service, ensuring compatibility of host and guest; young people are placed in homes with other young people of similar interests

Cost from £65 bed & breakfast, £75 half board, £85 full board, per week. Service charge £60.

Adults are met at local stations; young people can be met at airport/station at extra cost

Insurance arranged on request

H

FRANCE

Inter Séjours 179 rue de Courcelles, 75017 Paris, France

(33 1) 47 63 06 81

A non-profitmaking organisation founded in 1968, arranging homestays and linguistic stays

Homestays arranged in the Perpignan, Montpellier and Loire Valley regions. 2+ weeks, all year. Apply at least 2 months in advance.

Individuals, groups, families and adults

Ages 12+

Some knowledge of French desirable. Language courses available.

Outings arranged by families

Full board accommodation in single/shared bedrooms. Information about the host family is sent to the participant in advance, so that correspondence can take place beforehand if desired.

Cost from FF3,700 for 2 weeks. Registration fee FF250.

Participants are met at the nearest station

Insurance provided

Also arrange combined homestay/language/activity holidays and au pair placements

FRANCE, SPAIN

Intercultural Exchange Limited Haddon Close, Chillington, Ilminster, Somerset TA19 0PU

Ilminster (01460) 55136   Fax (01460) 55897

A commercial organisation established in 1983 to promote a better understanding of other countries through their language, culture and everyday life, both at home and in the workplace

Homestays arranged in France (Annecy, Nevers) and Spain (Tarragona, Salamanca). 5 days to 1 month, all year. Apply 2-3 weeks in advance.

Application forms are designed to extract the maximum information about participants, in order to make a good matching

Individuals, groups and adults

All ages from primary school upwards

Some knowledge of the relevant language may be required, depending on type of stay. Linguistic stays include 10-15 hours language tuition per week.

Activities and excursions are organised, and where possible, participation in local events

Full board accommodation in family home. Homes are visited by local centre supervisor, and families are vetted.

Cost from £120 per week, depending on type of stay

Return travel is included in fee. On linguistic stays children are escorted; 1 adult for 15 children. Participants met on arrival.

Standard travel insurance provided, to include health, theft and personal liability

Also offer school and college trips; work experience programmes

AUSTRIA, FRANCE, GERMANY, ITALY, MALTA, PORTUGAL, NETHERLANDS, RUSSIA, SPAIN, SWEDEN

International Language Homestays 2 Cecil Square, Margate, Kent CT9 1BD

Thanet (01843) 227700 Fax (01843) 223377

A commercial organisation set up in 1989 organising immersion language courses where students live with, and are taught by their own teacher

Participants can learn French in France, German in Germany and Austria, Italian in Italy, Spanish in Spain, Portuguese in Portugal, Dutch in the Netherlands, Swedish in Sweden, English in Malta and Russian in Russia. 1+ weeks, all year.

Individuals, families and adults

Ages 16+ for Russia, otherwise no age limits

Each course is tailor-made with 15, 20 or 25 hours tuition per week

Students are fully integrated into the social life and activities of the family. Living with the language teacher means students are guided and corrected not only during lessons but also when accompanying the teacher on family activities and excursions. If sufficient notice is given students can be placed with teachers who share their interests.

Full board accommodation in teacher's family home. Sharing programme available if two participants wish to book together.

Costs vary according to location and tuition. Private tuition and full board accommodation from £285 per week.

Transfers can be arranged to/from host teacher's home at extra cost

Insurance not provided

FRANCE, GERMANY, ITALY, RUSSIA / FORMER SOVIET UNION, SPAIN

International Links 145 Manygate Lane, Shepperton, Middlesex TW17 9EP

Walton-on-Thames (01932) 229300   Fax (01932) 222294

A commercial organisation set up in 1988 to promote language learning through homestays

Homestays arranged in France (Paris, Loire Valley, Abbeville, Brittany, La Rochelle, South of France), Germany (Berlin, Brühl, Cologne, Munster, Bocholt, Bergan, Celle), Italy (Rome, Siena), Spain (Madrid, Cadiz, Alicante, Puerto de Santa Maria) and Russia/Former Soviet Union (St Petersburg, Moscow, Minsk). 1-4 weeks, all year.

Individuals only

No age limits; depends on individual requirements

Applicants should have an interest in the language and the culture of the country to be visited. Language tuition can be arranged in most places at £16 per hour.

Excursions to places of interest can be arranged

Full board accommodation. Single room in family home. Families are visited by a contact in the host country to ensure high standards.

Cost approx £180 per week

Transfers can be arranged at extra cost

Insurance can be provided

Also offer summer schools in France and Russia

H

FRANCE, GERMANY

Interspeak Ltd The Coach House, Blackwood Estate, Blackwood, Lanarkshire ML11 0JG

Lanark (01555) 894219   Fax (01555) 894954

A commercial organisation founded in 1981 to provide good family accommodation for foreign students and to improve international relationships among young people

Homestays arranged in France (Paris, La Rochelle, Brittany, Normandy, Poitou-Charentes) and Germany. 1+ weeks, all year.

Individuals, groups, families, adults

Ages 12+

At least 2 years' study of French/German required. Language courses can be arranged.

Outings and organised activities available as part of language course in Paris and La Rochelle

Half board accommodation in family home with teenage children where possible. Single bedrooms.

Cost from £95 per week, accommodation only

Insurance not provided

H

NETHERLANDS

ISOK (Internationale-Studieverblijven Organisatie Katwijk)
Jan-Tooropstraat 4, 2225 XT Katwijk aan Zee, Netherlands

(31 1718) 13533

A commercial organisation set up in 1967 with the aim of teaching Dutch to foreigners and bringing them into contact with Dutch culture, people, landscapes and way of life

Homestays mainly in the region between Haarlem and Rotterdam, an area noted for the purity of its spoken Dutch. 1+ weeks, all year.

Individuals, groups and adults

No age limits

No previous knowledge of Dutch necessary, just a willingness to learn. Language tuition available, cost Dfl 15, 2 hours in small groups; or Dfl 25 per hour, private tuition.

Host families organise weekend excursions

Full board accommodation in a Dutch family. Normally in single rooms, unless children wish to share with a Dutch child of similar age.

Cost Dfl 315 per week covers meals, accommodation and linguistic help from the host family. Dfl 50 registration fee.

Guests are met at Leiden railway station or Schiphol-Amsterdam airport by host family and/or ISOK staff

Insurance not provided

H

ESTONIA , LATVIA , LITHUANIA , KAZAKHSTAN , RUSSIA , UKRAINE , UZBEKISTAN

MIR Corporation 85 South Washington Street, Suite 210, Seattle, Washington 98104, United States

(1 206) 624 7289   Fax (1 206) 624 7360

A commercial company established in 1986 to arrange and promote specialised travel to countries in the Former Soviet Union and Central Europe. Works in partnership with grassroots citizen and ecology groups in the Former Soviet Union who are working towards real democratic change.

Homestays arranged mainly in Moscow, St Petersburg and Kiev, but also available in Irkutsk, Novosibirsk, Tashkent and cities in the Baltic States. Stays available year round; duration according to requirements. Recommended to apply 60 days in advance.

Individuals, groups, families and adults

No age limits

Knowledge of foreign languages not required. Each host family includes at least one English-speaker. Russian language tape and booklet provided, plus country orientation manual.

Variety of activities can be arranged, from tourist excursions to specialised counterpart meetings, depending on requirements

Half-board accommodation in family apartments; single/double rooms, shared bathroom. In most cases, representatives interview families and visit homes before booking is made. Effort made to match client's profession/interests with those of the host.

Cost from $55 per person per night double occupancy

Participants arrange own travel; visas arranged at extra cost. Guests met on arrival at train station or airport and returned there upon departure.

Insurance cover can be arranged at extra charge

Also arrange hotel accommodation in Former Soviet Union and Central Europe; summer language courses at the Pushkin Institute in Moscow

FRANCE

Le Nonante Famille d'Accueil, chez Mme Geneviève Dhommée, 90 rue Mirabeau, 37000 Tours, France

(33) 47 05 34 83   Fax (33) 47 05 34 83

A private family organisation which since 1980 has been hosting foreign students who go to France to study the language

Homestays arranged in Tours. 1-9 months, all year. Apply at least 3 months in advance.

Individuals and groups

No age limits

In order to improve language learning, those staying in the family are required to speak French at all times. French courses are available at local language schools, including the Institut de Touraine, the Institut Européen de Français and at the university.

Excursions can be arranged through a local company, or with the family and friends. Discussion evenings held with local people.

Half or full board accommodation; single or double rooms. Up to 11 students can be accommodated at any one time.

Cost varies depending on season, from FF3,600 per month for half board in double room

Guests make their own travel arrangements, but can be met on arrival if necessary

All guests must be covered by their own personal insurance

MALTA

NSTS Student and Youth Travel 220 St Paul Street, Valletta, Malta

(356) 244983/246628

A non-profitmaking organisation founded in 1955 to provide young people with the opportunity of widening their knowledge and education through travel, contacts and exchanges

Homestays arranged in residential areas of Sliema and suburbs. 1 week-3 months, all year; ages 30+ September-June only.

Individuals, groups, families and adults

Ages 12-30+

English courses arranged

In addition to those activities arranged by the host family, day excursions, leisure activities and sports are organised regularly June-September, or on request during the winter

Full board accommodation; single/twin bedrooms in family home

Cost LM42 or LM50 (June-September) per week, full board including one cultural activity/excursion

Escorted travel provided for groups of 25+

Insurance provided on request

Also arrange arts, crafts and computer courses, all year

FIYTO

RUSSIA

Obninsk Humanities Centre Lara Putsello, 7 St David's Road, Ramsgate, Kent CT11 7EP

Thanet (01843) 588736 or 0181-855 0629

A non-profitmaking organisation set up in 1990 to run tours and homestays in Obninsk, a quiet, green town within easy reach of Moscow, and ideal as a base to discover the real Russia of today.

Homestays arranged in Obninsk, 60 miles from Moscow. 10+ days, all year. Apply at least 1 month in advance.

Individuals, groups, families and adults

No age limits

Knowledge of Russian not essential. English-speaking hosts and interpreters available; programme can include Russian tuition.

Sightseeing excursions arranged. Horse riding, gym, swimming pool and bike rental available.

Full board accommodation in family home. Single/twin rooms. Host families are carefully selected for comfort, cleanliness and a friendly atmosphere.

Cost from £300 for 10 days (for groups of at least 7) includes accommodation, transfer to and from Moscow airport, activities, services of guide/interpreter and three 1-hour Russian lessons, if desired

Air travel arranged by Progressive Tours Ltd at extra cost. Participants are met on arrival, and an escort is provided for all travel within Russia.

Insurance cover can be arranged at extra cost

Also arrange Russian language courses; boarding school programmes for ages 13-16

FRANCE

Offairte UK Ltd Victoria House, Victoria Street, Taunton, Somerset TA1 3JA

Taunton (01823) 334373

A commercial organisation established in 1988 and specialising in education and language travel. Live n' Learn programme aims to immerse students in their target language by accommodating them in their tutor's home or with a selected host family close by.

Participants can study French in the Bayonne, Biarritz and Pau regions. 2, 3 or 4 weeks, all year. Apply at least 6 weeks in advance.

Individuals only

Ages 15+

Elementary level of French required. 15, 20 or 25 hours language tuition per week.

Students are included in family activities and outings. Additional activities and excursions can be arranged at extra cost.

Full board accommodation in tutor's home or with nearby family. Single bedroom. All tutors are interviewed in their homes, which are inspected by the Director of Studies or a local representative.

Cost for 2 weeks from £830 (15 hours per week) to £1,395 (25 hours per week). All course materials and tourist information provided.

Participants arrange and pay for own travel. Ages 15-16 are met at the airport and accompanied to tutor's home. Adults are met at local coach/rail station by tutor or local representative.

Insurance not provided

GERMANY

OIK (Organisation für Internationale Kontakte) Postfach 201 051, Alte Bahnhofstraße 26, Bad Godesberg, 53140 Bonn 2, Germany

(49 228) 356076   Fax (49 228) 364368

A non-profitmaking organisation established in 1975 to promote international understanding between Germany and other countries through international meetings, study and special interest tours and homestay programmes

Homestays arranged throughout Germany. 3 nights-2 months, all year.

Groups only

Ages 10-26

Knowledge of German helpful but not essential. Homestays can be combined with language courses.

Sightseeing excursions, official receptions, river cruises and visits to places of interest can be arranged depending on group requirements

Full board accommodation in carefully selected families. One or two guests per family.

Costs depend on length of programmes and requirements. For example, DM395, 7 nights includes full board and programme of excursions. For groups of 20+, group leader takes part free.

Insurance can be provided

Also arrange study tours, specialised tours for sports groups or school bands, international youth music festivals, city packages and budget tours

H

AUSTRIA

ÖKISTA (Österreichisches Komitee für Internationalen Studienaustausch) Garnisongasse 7, 1090 Vienna, Austria

(43 1) 40148/225   Fax (43 1) 40148290

A non-profitmaking organisation founded in 1950 by the Austrian government, serving the youth and student community of Austria as well as many individuals and groups from other countries

Homestays arranged in most Austrian cities. 3+ weeks, all year.

Individuals, groups and families

Ages 18-30

Previous knowledge of German not essential

No activities arranged

Bed & breakfast accommodation in family homes. Single/shared rooms.

Cost AS160 per day; registration fee AS500

Travel is the client's responsibility

Insurance not provided

Also offer German language courses, camps and international youth holiday centres, au pair visits, sightseeing/study tours, and a youth travel and accommodation service

FIYTO

FRANCE

PGL School Tours Alton Court, Penyard Lane, Ross-on-Wye, Herefordshire HR9 5NR

Ross-on-Wye (01989) 764342   Fax (01989) 768376

A commercial organisation founded in 1957, offering a wide range of tailor-made educational holidays and tours for groups

Homestays arranged in the Paris suburbs, Loire Valley, La Rochelle and Le Havre

Groups only

Ages 11+

At least a rudimentary understanding of French necessary

Complete programme of excursions organised

Full board accommodation in single/twin bedrooms, carefully inspected by local organisers. Families are chosen for their readiness to accommodate English schoolchildren, and wherever possible participants are placed with families who have children of a similar age.

Cost from £210-£224 based on 35 pupils spending 7 days in Saumur. Prices increase considerably for Paris, Le Havre and La Rochelle.

Return coach/ferry travel from school or college to destination provided

Insurance included

PGL Young Adventure arrange activity and sports holidays for individuals, groups and families

ABTA SAGTA

FORMER SOVIET UNION

Room With The Russians Lynton Cooper Travel (London) Ltd, Station Chambers, High Street North, London E6 1JE

0181-472 2694

A commercial tour operator established in 1974 which has recently linked up with a Russian independent travel organisation catering especially for individuals wishing to stay in people's homes

Homestays arranged in Moscow, St Petersburg and Kiev. Most stays include a few nights in two of these cities. 7, 10 or 14 nights, February-December. Weekend stays in Moscow and St Petersburg also available.

Individuals and groups

Ages 12+

Knowledge of Russian not required

Stays include city tours; range of optional trips to places of interest

Accommodation in private twin or double bedroom in family home, sharing bathroom facilities. Usually only breakfast is provided, however some hosts offer evening meals at extra cost. All host families are carefully chosen, and are people who enjoy receiving guests in their homes. Each participant is provided with guide books, maps and detailed information on restaurants, currency and healthcare.

Cost varies, depending on season, length of stay and cities visited. For example, a tour of 7 nights in St Petersburg or Moscow costs from £460 inclusive. Visa charge £16. Single room supplement £9 per person per night.

Return flight from Britain and air/rail transport within the FSU included in cost. Guests are met on arrival and taken by car to host's home.

Insurance can be arranged

Also offer furnished apartments for leasing; a service for independent travellers wishing to set up their own itineraries is anticipated

BELGIUM, FRANCE, GERMANY, ITALY, RUSSIA, SPAIN

SEE Europe Ltd Outbound Division, I Church Walk Studios, Beales Lane, Weybridge, Surrey KT13 8JS

Weybridge (01932) 840440   Fax (01932) 856514

A private organisation set up in 1974 to add an extra dimension to language learning by promoting homestays as a way of experiencing and understanding other peoples' lifestyles and culture

Homestays from 3-14 nights. France: Paris, Brittany, Normandy, Pas de Calais, Loire Valley, Provence, Limousin, Poitou-Charente, Champagne, Alsace, French Riviera. Germany: Rhineland, Berlin, Potsdam, Bavaria, Schleswig-Holstein, Hesse. Spain: Castille Leon, Andalucia, Cantabria, Catalonia, Valencia, Rioja. Italy: Rome, Naples, Milan. Belgium: Brussels. Russia: Moscow and St Petersburg.

Groups and individuals

Ages 10-20. Can cater for school/college and adult learning groups.

Basic knowledge of the relevant language required. Group homestay programmes may include lessons with native tutors and afternoon cultural excursions. Full range of courses offered to individuals.

Excursions arranged during group stays. Sports available.

Full board accommodation with packed lunch on excursion days. Twin rooms mostly; maximum 2 per family.

Costs vary according to destination, duration, group size and programme. For example, 2 week homestay in Paris from £470 (reductions for groups).

Groups travel by coach and ferry or by air, and are met at destination by local coordinator

Insurance included in all programmes

ABTA FIYTO SAGTA

FRANCE

SILC (Séjours Internationaux Linguistiques et Culturels)
32 Rempart de l'Est, 16022 Angoulême Cedex, France

(33) 45 97 41 00   Fax (33) 45 95 41 10

A non-profitmaking organisation founded in 1965, aiming to develop skills in the educational field whilst favouring greater cultural interchange

Mrs F Forrest-Evans, 50 Cypress Avenue, Whitton, Middlesex TW2 7JZ
℃ 0181-894 1511

Homestays arranged in the Paris region, Orléans, Limousin, Le Havre, Biarritz, Montpellier, Perpignan, Royan, Grenoble, Côte d'Azur, Bordeaux and Angoulême. 2+ weeks, all year, but mostly Christmas, Easter and summer vacations.

Individuals, groups and adults

All ages

Basic knowledge of French necessary. Personalised language courses on request.

Sports, activities, group excursions and visits arranged on request

Local organisers select host families and match them with participants; single/twin bedrooms.

Cost FF1,520-FF4,280 per week full board, depending on location; FF240 registration fee

Escorted travel can be arranged; participants can be met at stations/ports

Insurance provided

Also arrange cultural/sightseeing tours, study tours, in-service training courses and au pair placements

H but no facilities for wheelchairs   **FIYTO FIOCES**

ENGLAND

Academic Travel (Lowestoft) Ltd The Briar School of English, 8 Gunton Cliff, Lowestoft, Suffolk NR32 4PE

Lowestoft (01502) 573781   Fax (01502) 589150

A commercial organisation founded in 1958, aiming to promote contact and travel among overseas people by assisting them to experience and enjoy the English way of life

Homestays arranged in Lowestoft, on the Norfolk coast. 2+ weeks, Easter and summer.

Individuals and groups

Ages 12-21

All levels of English accepted. English language courses available.

Sports, excursions, social programme available; most families arrange outings

Full board accommodation in family home. Host families are visited and interviewed by accommodation and welfare officers to ensure that family and home meet set standards. 24 hour welfare service for immediate complaints/problems.

Cost from £155 per week

Transfers by couriers from ports on certain days

Insurance not provided

IRELAND

Andrews Travel Consultants Ltd Rockford House, Deansgrange Road, Black Rock, Co Dublin, Ireland

Dublin (353 1) 2845512 Fax (353 1) 2807525

A private organisation founded in 1969 aiming to provide tourism in Ireland, organising a variety of holidays including private homestays

Homestays arranged in Dublin, Bray, Galway and other areas on request. 1+ weeks, all year.

Individuals, groups, families and adults

Ages 12+

English language courses arranged in Dublin and provincial centres

Tours and sports activities provided

Bed and breakfast, half or full board accommodation in carefully selected families; single/twin bedrooms

Costs, on request, vary according to areas and terms

Insurance not provided

Also arrange farmhouse, sports/activity and combined English language/activity holidays, summer camps and study courses

H

ENGLAND

Anglo-Italian Holidays 44 Kyrle Road, London SW11 6BA

0171-978 4926

A private organisation set up in 1985 to help young Italians and Britons visit each other's country and sample each other's way of life

Homestays arranged in the London suburbs of Battersea, Clapham, Fulham, Putney, Wimbledon and Hammersmith; also in Cambridge and in country districts of Essex, Gloucestershire, Norfolk, Suffolk and Worcestershire. Length of stay to suit individual requirements, but country stays are only available during July and August.

Individuals and adults

Ages 12-17 for country areas; 17+ for London areas

Previous knowledge of English not necessary. English language courses can be arranged.

No special activities arranged in London. Riding, swimming, sailing, tennis, barbecues and outings arranged by families in country areas.

Bed and breakfast (with use of kitchen) or half-board accommodation in family homes. Full board offered in country homes. Single room, unless two friends wish to share.

Cost £70-£80 bed & breakfast, £100-£110 half board per week (single room) or £55-£65 bed & breakfast, £85-£90 half board per week (double room). Country stays £220-£250 per week, full board. Registration fee £90.

Children met at airport on arrival and returned to airport on departure. Other participants make their own travel arrangements.

Insurance not provided

Also arrange au pair stays in England and Italy

ENGLAND, IRELAND

Animations Loisirs Jeunes   58 bis, rue Sala, 69002 Lyon, France

(33) 72 40 96 42   Fax (33) 78 37 57 56

A non-profitmaking organisation set up in 1971, arranging activity holidays, linguistic stays, total immersion homestays and exchanges

Homestays arranged in Basingstoke, Skegness, Chelmsford and Dublin suburbs. 2-3 weeks, July and August.

Individuals and groups

Ages 8-18, depending on area

Basic knowledge of English required. Language courses included in most programmes except total immersion, where children are in a totally English-speaking environment.

Excursions, sporting activities and visits to places of interest included in most programmes. Families also organise activities.

Full board accommodation in selected families; only one French child per family. Usually there will be a child in the host family of the same age.

Cost FF6,500-FF8,050 depending on length of stay and activities; FF80 registration fee

Escorted travel provided from Lyon, by train, coach, ferry or plane depending on destination. One group leader per 20 children; group leader remains during the whole stay.

Insurance provided

Also arrange linguistic stays for French children in Germany, Spain, United States and Canada; activity holidays

ENGLAND, IRELAND

Aquitaine Service Linguistique 6 Rue Pasteur, 33127 Martignas, France

(33) 56 21 40 96 Fax (33) 56 78 04 01

A non-profitmaking organisation founded in 1978 arranging homestays, and language courses

Homestays arranged in south London, Brighton/Hove, Essex, Kent and Dublin areas. England: 1+ weeks, all year; Ireland: 2+ weeks, all year.

Individuals, families, groups and adults

Ages 12+, England, depending on location; ages 14+, Ireland

All levels of English accepted. Combined homestay/languagecourses available in most areas.

Cultural/sports facilities available in most areas

Single/shared bedrooms in carefully selected families of similar backgrounds and interests, with children of same age where appropriate. Farmstays available in Ireland.

England: cost from FF1,690 1 week, FF2,780 2 weeks, full board. Ireland: cost from FF2,980 2 weeks, full board. Registration fee FF180.

Help given with travel arrangements; transfers included for stays in Dublin

Insurance provided

Also offer language courses, exchanges between France/United States

ENGLAND, SCOTLAND, WALES

Aunties (Great Britain) Limited 56 Coleshill Terrace, Llanelli, Dyfed SA15 3DA

Llanelli (01554) 770077

A commercial agency set up in 1984 to help vegetarians worldwide find short-term accommodation in pleasant British homes with hosts sympathetic to their guests' chosen way of eating. Non-vegetarians also welcome.

Homestays arranged in the London suburbs and throughout England, Scotland and Wales. Up to 6 weeks, all year.

Individuals, groups (south Wales only), families and adults

No age limits but those under 18 must be accompanied

Knowledge of English not necessary. Language tuition can be arranged.

Excursions and activities arranged for groups or students on full board

Bed & breakfast or full board accommodation in family homes

Cost £13-£17 per night bed & breakfast or £140 per week full board for individuals. £17 per day full board for groups of 10 or more (south Wales only).

Escorted travel can be provided from airports to host home at extra cost

Insurance not provided

ENGLAND, SCOTLAND

Avalon Student Travel 11 Marlborough Place, Brighton, Sussex BN1 1UB

Brighton (01273) 553417   Fax (01273) 559321

A commercial organisation founded in 1963 with the aim of providing a personal service enabling young people to have a low-cost holiday learning English in a family

Homestays arranged in Brighton/Hove and surrounding area; towns and villages in Sussex; Edinburgh, London and York. 1+ weeks, individuals, 3+ days, groups.

Individuals and groups

Ages 15+ individuals; 12+ groups

At least a basic knowledge of English desirable; language tuition can be arranged at associate study centre

Families will sometimes arrange outings; excursion programme for groups

Accommodation in family home. All host families are visited and inspected. Students are sent a description of the family and details of the accommodation offered. 24 hour emergency telephone service; accommodation secretary available to investigate any problems and to offer advice during stay.

Cost £70 half-board, £77.50 full board (suburbs only) per week. Single room supplement £10 per week. Reductions for groups.

Escorted travel arrangements for individuals available at extra cost. Groups can be met on arrival at ports/airports with coach transport.

Insurance arranged on request

ENGLAND

Belaf Study Holidays Banner Lodge, Cherhill, Calne, Wiltshire SN11 8XR

Calne (01249) 812551   Fax (01249) 821 533

A professional organisation set up in 1975 by language teachers, and specialising in total immersion homestays for children and adults. Registered in France with the Ministère de Jeunesse et de Sports.

Homestays arranged in central and southern England throughout the year

Individuals and groups

Ages 8+

Previous knowledge of English not essential but desirable. An individual home study programme is provided and a teacher visits weekly to correct the work.

Sports and leisure activities and at least one excursion per week provided by the host family

Full board accommodation in carefully selected families, chosen to match interests and requirements

Cost from £150 per week plus travel

Escorted travel in school holidays from France (Nice, Lyon, Paris, Brittany, Normandy); Switzerland (Geneva); and Spain (Barcelona). Children are met by the host family at point of arrival.

Insurance included

H

ENGLAND

Castle Holiday Homes I New Inn Lane, Guildford, Surrey GU4 7HN

Guildford (01483) 32345

A private organisation founded in 1958 organising leisure and cultural activities for short stay groups and adult tours

Homestays arranged in Bognor Regis, Chichester, Guildford, Havant, Southbourne and Woking. I+ weeks during holidays for individuals; 3+ days for groups, who should apply at least 3 months in advance.

Individuals, groups, families and adults

Ages 14+

Elementary level of English required. Language courses available at centres in Chichester, Guildford, Southbourne and Woking.

Sports and excursions arranged

Full board accommodation in single/twin/double bedrooms in selected families

Cost £112 per week, individuals; £12.50 per day, short stay groups; £15 per day, adult groups

Escorted travel provided from airport for under 18s. Coaches provided for group transfers if required.

Insurance not provided

Also arrange special interest tours for groups of aviation enthusiasts, ages 16+

H

ENGLAND, WALES

Country Cousins Ltd Channel School, Bicclescombe, Ilfracombe, Devon EX34 8JN

Ilfracombe (01271) 862834/863304   Fax (01271) 865374

A commercial organisation founded in 1956 arranging English language programmes and homestays in selected families

Homestays arranged throughout the West Country, Gwent and Powys. Usually 3 weeks, all year.

Individuals, groups, families, and adults

All ages

Minimum of elementary English required. Language tuition available through Stay with an English Teacher programme.

Outings with the host family

Full board accommodation in approved families. The aim is to match age and interests of the guest with those of the family.

Cost from £328, 2 weeks. Stay with an English Teacher programme cost from £585, 2 weeks.

Escort service available from Heathrow, with coach service to the West Country

Insurance available; cost £15 for 28 days

Also offer language courses with excursions/activities, spring and summer

H

ENGLAND

Cultural Travel International 13A Cranley Gardens, London SW7 3BB

0171-373 0791   Fax 0171-373 6960

A commercial organisation founded in 1982, offering a student travel service

Homestays arranged in Bournemouth, Canterbury, York, Tunbridge Wells, Worcester and London (Catford and Harrow). 2 days-4 weeks, all year.

Individuals, groups and families

Ages 12-23

No previous knowledge of English required. Linguistic stays available in Canterbury and Worcester, 2-4 weeks during the summer.

Outings may be arranged by the host family. Excursions arranged for groups.

Full board accommodation in family home. Families are carefully selected and have background and interests to fit in with those of guests. Single room for individuals; for groups a maximum of 2 participants are placed with each family.

Cost from £100-£150 per week, individuals, depending on location and facilities. Linguistic stays £165-£175 per week. Special rates for groups.

Individuals can be transferred from designated pick-up point, cost from £40. Coach transfer for groups.

Insurance not provided

ENGLAND

Dragons International The Old Vicarage, South Newington, Banbury, Oxfordshire OX15 4JN

Banbury (01295) 721717   Fax (01295) 721991

A commercial organisation founded in 1975 and specialising in individual exchanges and homestays

Dragons International, 16 rue de la Chapelle, 78630 Orgeval, France ℂ (33) 39 75 53 40

Homestays arranged throughout England. 2 weeks, July-August.

Individuals only

Ages 11-19

Basic knowledge of English required

Host families arrange outings

Full board accommodation; single/shared rooms in carefully selected families having young people of similar age or background

Cost FF200 per day to cover cost of accommodation

Escorted coach travel from a number of pick-up points in France provided, from FF2,000 depending on point of departure

Insurance provided

UNOSEL

BRITAIN

En Famille Agency (Britain) 50 Somerset Road, East Preston, West Sussex BN16 1BY

Arundel (01903) 783636   Fax (01903) 783630

A private company founded in 1945 offering holidays for travellers wishing to learn or practise English in private family homes in Britain

Homestays arranged throughout Britain. 1+ weeks, all year.

Individuals, groups, families and adults

Ages 5+

All levels of English catered for. Language tuition can be arranged.

Guests take part in family outings

Half or full board accommodation in family homes. Host families are all personally inspected. Particular care is taken to match the family with the individual's requirements, details of background, interests and facilities being carefully compared. Both applicants and host family must provide two references.

Cost £100-£160 half board, £110-£270 full board, per week; registration fee £16; selection and booking fee £26.

Escorted travel arranged on request. Host families or representative can meet visitors at airport/station at extra cost.

Insurance provided

ENGLAND

English Family Experience 3 Lower Marlands, Bromley Cross, Bolton, Lancashire BL7 9HG

Bolton (01204) 594147

A small, family-run company established in 1992, specialising in bringing students to the north of England to improve their English and promote long-term friendships with English families

Homestays arranged in Bolton, northwest England. 1-4 weeks, all year. Recommended to apply 3 months in advance.

An effort is made to match student's hobbies and interests with those of the host family

Individuals and groups

Ages 16-24

Two year's knowledge of English required. 15 hours per week English tuition provided.

Programme includes excursions, meals out and evening entertainments

Full board accommodation in family home. Lunch provided during language tuition/excursions.

Cost £115 per week (October-April) or £150 per week (May-September)

Participants met on arrival at Manchester airport/train or bus station and escorted to host family home

Insurance not provided

ENGLAND

English Host Holidays 21 Manor Way, Hayling Island, Hampshire PO11 9JH

Hayling Island (01705) 462191   Fax (01705) 468227

A private organisation established in 1989 to provide a range of linguistic stays and holidays

Homestays arranged at Hayling Island, just off the Hampshire coast. Length and dates of stay to suit requirements.

Individuals, groups, families and adults

No age limits

No previous knowledge of English required. English language tuition can be arranged.

Variety of excursions, sports and leisure activities available

Half-board accommodation in host family, plus packed lunch; single/ shared room. Each family is checked for suitability.

Cost from £10.50 per person per night

Pick up may be arranged from airport/ferry terminal if required

Insurance not provided

Also offer residential accommodation for groups; business English tuition

H

ENGLAND

English Language and Leisure 7B Avalanche Road, Southwell, Portland, Dorset DT5 2DJ

Portland (01305) 820735   Fax (01305) 860032

A commercial organisation set up in 1989 arranging homestays, linguistic stays, sports, sightseeing and activity programmes

Homestays arranged in Weymouth and Portland. Length of stay to suit individual requirements. Apply 1 month in advance.

Families have background and interests to fit in with those of guests

Individuals, groups, families, adults

Ages 10+

Previous knowledge of English not necessary. English language courses available for groups or as 1:1 tuition.

Activities and excursions included in group programmes. Windsurfing, sailing and horse riding courses available.

Bed & breakfast, half board or full board accommodation in carefully selected family homes. Single/twin bedroom. All families are visited to ensure high standards.

Cost £12 per person per night, bed & breakfast; £17 full board. Reductions for groups. Course rates on request.

Escorted travel can be arranged. Groups are met on arrival; individuals met on request.

Insurance not provided

IRELAND

English Language Professionals Brunswick House, Brunswick Place, Dublin 2, Ireland

(353 1) 667 5111

A commercial, cooperative company established in 1993 to provide 1:1 home tuition English courses for business and professional people

Courses available in Dublin, Galway, Sligo, Adare, Waterford, Kerry, Kilkenny and other rural and seaside locations throughout Ireland. 2+ days, all year. 3 weeks notice preferred.

Student and teacher are matched according to personalities, talents, family circumstances and location.

Individuals, families and adults

Mainly adults, but some teachers cater for 12-18 age group

Programme includes 15-30 hours per week English language tuition, on a 1:1 basis, tuned to the individual needs of the student

Excursions and other activities can be arranged at extra cost. For those on an English for Special Purposes (ESP) course, relevant professional or business outings can be arranged.

Full board accommodation in the teacher's home; private room. 12-16 year-olds are placed in families who have children in the same age group. All teacher-hosts are company shareholders; their homes are inspected and must conform to the company's quality standards.

Prices range from £500 per week for 15 hours of general English to £950 per week for 30 hours, ESP.

Participants are met on arrival; nominal pick-up charge of £15

Insurance not provided

ENGLAND

Euro-Academy Ltd 77a George Street, Croydon, Surrey CR0 1LD

0181-681 2905/6   Fax 0181-681 8850

A private organisation founded in 1971 to develop the relationships between young people by bringing them together on both study and activity courses

Homestays arranged in Greater London, Kent, Berkshire, Oxfordshire, Yorkshire, Sussex, the West Country, Cambridge, Chester and the Lake District. 1+ weeks, all year.

Individuals and groups

Ages 10-35

Knowledge of English helpful but not essential. English language/activity courses can be arranged.

Excursions and sports courses available

Full board accommodation in carefully selected families; single/twin bedrooms

Cost £125-£150 per week, depending on location and facilities

Escorted travel can be arranged

Insurance not provided

ABTA FIYTO SAGTA

ENGLAND, IRELAND

European Educational Opportunities Programme 28 Canterbury Road, Lydden, Dover, Kent CT15 7ER

Dover (01304) 830948/823631   Fax (01304) 831914/825869

A non-profitmaking organisation founded in 1986 aiming to offer high-quality programmes through carefully selected homes, schools and allied agencies

Homestays arranged in southern England, East Anglia, Cornwall, Yorkshire and southern Ireland. 2+ weeks, all year.

Individuals, groups, families and adults

Ages 12+

Basic knowledge of English desirable. English conversation classes available in most areas; homestays combined with formal tuition available in Kent and Sussex, Easter and summer.

Outings usually arranged by the families; homestays with organised excursions available for ages 15+

Full board accommodation in family home. Students are totally integrated into the family. Students aged 12-18 are supervised by a member of staff; parents may telephone at any time to discuss problems or areas of concern.

Cost from £128 per week

Participants are met on arrival at Dover or Folkestone; escorted travel can be arranged

Insurance not provided

H

ENGLAND

Euroyouth Ltd 301 Westborough Road, Westcliff, Southend-on-Sea, Essex SS0 9PT

Southend-on-Sea (01702) 341434 Fax (01702) 330104

A commercial organisation founded in 1961 with the aim of offering facilities for young people to practise the language which they are learning in a family setting and to experience the way of life of the country they are visiting

Homestays arranged in Essex and London. Length of stay according to individual requirements.

Individuals, groups, families and adults; individuals only in London

Ages 14+

Basic knowledge of English required. English language courses can be arranged; multi-national courses available July/August, courses for groups arranged all year.

Family outings at extra cost. Sports courses in July and August; weekly day outings. Visits and programmes arranged for groups.

Bed & breakfast, half or full board accommodation in selected and inspected family homes. Welfare service available, advice and assistance provided during stay if required.

Cost £96-£120 per week, depending on terms

Escorted travel arranged on request at extra cost

Insurance not provided; all guests must have personal liability cover

Also offer tailor made programmes for groups

H FIYTO FIOCES

BRITAIN, IRELAND

The Experiment in International Living Otesaga, West Malvern Road, Malvern, Worcestershire WR14 4EN

Malvern (01684) 562577

A non-profitmaking educational travel organisation founded in 1936 with the aim of promoting understanding, friendship and respect between people from different cultural backgrounds

Homestays arranged throughout Britain and Ireland. 1-2 weeks, all year; longer stays for individuals on request. Apply 8-10 weeks in advance.

Individuals, groups, families, adults

Ages 16+

Basic conversational English required. Language courses can be arranged.

Families usually arrange outings. Activities and excursions included in group programmes. Professional courses arranged on request.

Full board accommodation, usually single room, depending on family. Families are carefully selected with the understanding that the aim is to allow individuals to experience a different way of life; the circumstances and beliefs of the host family may therefore differ from those of the participants.

Cost £147, 1 week; £228, 2 weeks. Rates for longer stays on request. Booking deposit £50.

Group travel arrangements can be made; host families will meet participants at nearest station if requested

Insurance not provided; participants must take out own cover

Also offer special interest and UK/US high school programmes. Over 40 offices worldwide; details from UK office.

BRITAIN

Families in Britain Martins Cottage, Martins Lane, Birdham, Chichester, Sussex PO20 7AU

Birdham (01243) 512222 Fax (01243) 511377

A commercial company founded in 1960 specialising in introducing overseas visitors to private families

Agents in Spain, France, Belgium and Germany; addresses on request

Homestays arranged throughout Britain. 1+ weeks, all year.

Individuals, groups (up to 8 persons), families, adults

All ages

Basic knowledge of English an advantage. English lessons on a private basis or at a language school can be arranged. Visitors are totally immersed in the English way of life.

Host families organise visits to London and local places of interest

Full board accommodation in family homes. Families are very carefully selected by matching ages, interests, hobbies and background.

Cost £182-£224 per week. Registration fee approx £38.

Visitors can be met at air/sea ports at extra cost

Insurance not provided

Also arrange sports and special interest courses

H

GREAT BRITAIN

No. not available

Family Connections Dales Cottage, Haselbech Hill, Northampton NN6 9LL

Northampton (01604) 686294   Fax (01604) 686270

A private organisation established in 1992 to provide paying guest accommodation for students and adults wanting to visit Great Britain and improve their knowledge of English

Homestays arranged in London, Oxford, Cambridge and in country areas throughout Great Britain. 1+ weeks, all year. Apply at least 1 month in advance.

Hosts and guests are matched on the basis of interests, hobbies, likes and dislikes

Individuals, small groups, families and adults

Ages 12+

Basic knowledge of English required. English lessons can be arranged at a cost of £12-£15 per hour.

Depending on interests of guests, sightseeing and sports activities can be included with full board

Bed & breakfast, half or full board accommodation provided in host families; own bedroom with bathroom for adults; children may prefer to share. All host families are carefully selected and inspected.

Cost £25-£35 per night bed & breakfast; £100-£180 per week half board; £150-£250 per week full board. Registration fee £50.

Host families will meet guests from airports (fee charged if not local) or from bus or railway stations

Insurance not provided

ENGLAND, SCOTLAND

Florentina Bureau 9 Tower Road, Orpington, Kent BR6 0SG

Orpington (01689) 822875

A commercial organisation operating for over 20 years to provide linguistic and sightseeing holidays with sympathetic families

Homestays arranged in London and the home counties, Bath, Edinburgh and York. 2+ days, all year.

Individuals, groups (ages 18+), families and adults

All ages; those under 12 must be accompanied by an adult

No previous knowledge of English necessary. 15 hours language tuition per week organised for group stays.

Excursions and activities organised for group stays

Half board accommodation in family homes. Packed lunch optional. Single bedrooms for individuals; group stays are 2-3 per room.

Cost from £11.50 per person, per night

Guests can be met at point of arrival, cost £30

Insurance not provided

H

ENGLAND

GIJK Lingua International Ubierstraße 94, 53173 Bonn, Germany

(49 228) 957300   Fax (49 228) 9573040

A limited company founded in 1983, arranging a variety of international opportunities for young people

Homestays arranged in London. 1+ weeks, all year.

Individuals and groups

Ages 16+

Some knowledge of English desirable, but not essential

Excursions and activities can be arranged

Half board accommodation in family home. All families are visited and carefully selected.

Cost DM490 1 week, DM460 for each succeeding week

Help and advice can be given with travel arrangements

Insurance can be provided

Also arrange summer schools and courses; au pair stays worldwide

ENGLAND

GJW Education Services Southcote, Coreway, Sidmouth, Devon EX10 9SD

Sidmouth (01395) 515614   Fax (01395) 515614

A commercial organisation established in 1990 to promote language learning and international understanding through activity/language courses, homestays and term stays/academic year programmes

Homestays are arranged in south west England. 2+ weeks, all year. Apply 8 weeks in advance.

Hosts and guests are carefully matched according to interests and background

Individuals, groups, families and adults

Ages 9+

All levels of English accepted. English language courses available, or language tuition on a 1:1 basis with fully qualified tutor.

Host families organise visits to places of interest

Full board accommodation in family home; single/twin bedrooms. All homes are inspected, and families are required to submit references.

Cost from £155-£215 per week

Escorted travel can be arranged at extra cost. Host families collect from nearest bus or rail station.

Private medical insurance provided on request. All participants must have own travel insurance.

Also offer English and activity courses; term stays/year stays in independent schools and state grammar schools

H can cater for wheelchairs

ENGLAND, SCOTLAND, WALES, IRELAND

Home Language International Reservations Office, 17 Royal Crescent, Ramsgate, Kent CT11 9PE

Thanet (01843) 851116   Fax (01843) 590300

A commercial organisation set up in 1989, organising immersion language courses where students live with, and are taught by their own private teacher

Participants can study English in London, the south east, south west, Stratford-upon-Avon, Oxfordshire, Cambridgeshire, Manchester, York, Bournemouth; Edinburgh; and south Wales; and English or Gaelic in Dublin. 1+ weeks, all year. Apply 1 month in advance.

Individuals, adults and children

Ages 8+

No previous knowledge of language necessary. Usually 15, 20 or 25 hours language tuition per week.

Excursions and other activities can be provided, but usually at extra cost where, for example, entrance fees are involved

Full board accommodation in teacher's family home. Shared programme available where two students wish to learn together. Every effort made to match teacher's interests with those of the student. Organisers visit potential teachers to verify home and qualifications, and also contact students to monitor progress.

Costs vary according to intensity of tuition. For example, 1 week from £325 (15 hours tuition, shared) to £560 (25 hours tuition, 1:1).

Transfers can be arranged to and from teacher's home at extra cost

Insurance not provided

Also offer business and specialised vocabulary courses, and 5 star luxury specialised courses, on the same basis

H

BRITAIN

HOST (Hosting for Overseas Students) 18 Northumberland Avenue, London WC2N 5BJ

0171-925 2595

A charity founded in 1987 to introduce international students studying in Britain to British people, thereby increasing international friendship and understanding, and decreasing the students' loneliness and isolation

Homestays arranged throughout Britain. The scheme runs all year; students usually stay for a weekend, or 3-4 days over Easter and Christmas. Over 3,000 people so far have acted as hosts.

Individuals, families and adults

Ages 18+. Applicants must be international students studying full time at an institution in Britain.

The host is responsible for entertaining the student, and should involve them in their home life and any Christmas/Easter festivities

Full board accommodation. Hosts and guests are carefully matched.

No charge

Students make their own travel arrangements

Insurance not provided

H

BRITAIN

Host & Guest Service Harwood House, 27 Effie Road, London SW6 1EN

0171-731 5340   Fax 0171-736 7230

A private organisation founded in 1956, providing a wide variety of reliable accommodation with families according to individual needs

Homestays arranged throughout Britain. Length of stay to suit individual requirements.

Individuals, groups and families

All ages; young children will need to be accompanied by an adult

All language levels catered for. Details of local language schools provided on request.

Families may arrange outings

Offer an individual accommodation service, ensuring compatibility of host and guest; young people are placed in homes with young people of similar interests

Cost from £65 bed & breakfast, £75 half board, £80 full board, per week. Service charge £35.

Adults are met at local stations; young people can be met at airport/ station at extra cost

Insurance arranged on request

H

ENGLAND, IRELAND

Inter Séjours 179 rue de Courcelles, 75017 Paris, France

(33 1) 47 63 06 81

A non-profitmaking organisation founded in 1968, arranging homestays and linguistic stays

Homestays arranged in London, Cornwall and Cork, and on farms throughout England. 2+ weeks, all year. Apply at least 2 months in advance.

Individuals, groups, families and adults

Ages 14+

Some knowledge of English desirable. Language courses available.

Outings arranged by families

Full board accommodation in single/shared bedrooms. Information about the host family is sent to the participant in advance, so that correspondence can take place beforehand if desired.

Cost from FF3,800 (London, 2 weeks) to FF4,500 (Cork, 3 weeks)

Transfers can be arranged

Insurance provided

Also offer combined homestay/language/activity holidays and au pair placements

ENGLAND

Intercultural Exchange Limited Haddon Close, Chillington, Ilminster, Somerset TA19 0PU

Ilminster (01460) 55136   Fax (01460) 55897

A commercial organisation established in 1983 to promote a better understanding of other countries through their language, culture and everyday life, both at home and in the workplace

Homestays arranged in London and the towns of Bexhill, Folkestone and Maidstone. 5 days to 1 month, all year. Apply 2-3 weeks in advance.

Application forms are designed to extract the maximum information about participants, in order to make a good match

Individuals, groups and adults

All ages from primary school upwards

Some knowledge of English may be required, depending on type of stay. Linguistic stays include 10-15 hours English language tuition per week.

Activities and excursions are organised, and where possible, participation in local events

Full board accommodation in family home. Homes are visited by local centre supervisor, and families are vetted.

Cost from £120 per week, depending on type of stay

Return travel is included in fee. On linguistic stays children are escorted; 1 adult for 15 children. Participants are met on arrival.

Standard travel insurance provided, to include health, theft and personal liability

Also offer school and college trips; work experience programmes

H Special linguistic stay at Easter for blind/partially sighted children

ENGLAND, SCOTLAND, IRELAND

International Language Homestays 2 Cecil Square, Margate, Kent CT9 1BD

Thanet (01843) 227700 Fax (01843) 223377

A commercial organisation set up in 1989 organising immersion language courses where individual students live with, and are taught by their own private teacher.

Language homestays arranged throughout England, Scotland and Ireland. 1+ weeks all year.

Individuals families and adults

Ages 17+ for London, otherwise no age limits

Each course is tailor-made for the individual with 15, 20 or 25 hours language tuition per week

Students are fully integrated into the social life and activities of the family. Living with the language teacher means students are guided and corrected not only during lessons but also when accompanying the teacher on family activities and excursions. If sufficient notice is given students can be placed with teachers who share their interests.

Full board accommodation in teacher's family home. Special summer sharing programme available for young people where two students of similar age and level, but different nationalities, live and share lessons with the same teacher.

Costs vary according to location and tuition. Price for private tuition and full board accommodation from £340 per week.

Transfers can be arranged to and from host teacher's home at extra cost

Insurance not provided

ENGLAND, SCOTLAND

International Links 145 Manygate Lane, Shepperton, Middlesex TW17 9EP

Walton-on-Thames (01932) 229300   Fax (01932) 222294

A commercial organisation set up in 1988 to promote language learning through homestays

Homestays arranged throughout England and in Edinburgh and Glasgow. 1-4 weeks, all year.

Individuals only

No age limits; depends on individual requirements

Applicants should have some interest in English language and culture. Language tuition can be arranged in most places at £16 per hour.

Excursions to places of interest can be arranged

Full board accommodation. Single room in family home. Families are visited to ensure high standards.

Cost approx £180 per week

Transfers can be arranged at extra cost

Insurance can be provided

H

ENGLAND, SCOTLAND

Interspeak Ltd The Coach House, Blackwood Estate, Blackwood, Lanarkshire ML11 0JG

Lanark (01555) 894219   Fax (01555) 894954

A commercial organisation founded in 1981 to provide good family accommodation for foreign students and to improve international relationships among young people

Homestays arranged in England and Scotland. 1+ weeks, all year.

Work placement students, individuals, groups, families and adults

Ages 12+

Basic knowledge of English helpful. Combined homestay/language courses available. *Stages en enterprises*/work placements offered.

Outings arranged; organised activities available as part of the language course

Full or half board accommodation in a family home; single bedrooms

Cost from £95 per week

Participants can be met at airports at cost of £20

Insurance not provided

H

ENGLAND, SCOTLAND, WALES, IRELAND

InTuition Languages 109 Shepperton Road, London N1 3DF

0171-359 7794   Fax 0171-354 9613

A private company established in 1989 to provide total immersion courses combining homestay with formal language tuition, where students live and study in their teacher's home

Homestays arranged throughout the British Isles, in all major towns, city centres, in the countryside or by the sea. 1+ weeks, starting any Sunday in the year. Recommended to apply at least 1 month in advance.

A careful matching service is offered based on participant's age, interests, occupation, dietary requirements and choice of location

Individuals, groups, families and adults

Ages 16+

Basic knowledge of English required. Choice of 15, 20 or 25 hours' English tuition per week.

Families will integrate guests into their life, show them local places of interest and arrange sporting activities if required

Full board accommodation in teacher's family home; single room. Two-to-one programme available for two students wishing to learn together. Every host family is visited, inspected and interviewed.

Costs range from £499 to £637 per week, including tuition, accommodation and course materials

Arrangements to be met at point of arrival can be made for a nominal charge

All premises are covered for occupier's liability. Guests are requested to provide own personal insurance.

Also offer business and prestige language training

ENGLAND

Linden Bureau 68 Deanecroft Road, Eastcote, Pinner, Middlesex HA5 1SP

0181-866 5435   Fax 0181-866 0183

A private organisation founded in 1966, placing overseas visitors in families with an emphasis on personal attention

ICO, 55 rue de Rivoli, 75001 Paris, France

ARCE, via XX Settembre 2/44, 16121 Genova, Italy

Mrs M Noemia Carvalho, Rua Antonio José da Costa 47, 4100 Porto, Portugal

Associacion Internacional Cultural Au-Pair, Paseo de Gracia, 86, 6° 7ª, 08008 Barcelona, Spain

Mrs Ingrid Wilson, rue de la Promenade, 2105 Travers (Neuchâtel), Switzerland

Homestays arranged in the London areas of Pinner, Harrow, Ealing and Acton. 1+ weeks, all year.

Individuals, groups, families and adults

Ages 15+

Some knowledge of English preferred. Can provide advice on courses.

Excursions sometimes arranged by host family

Accommodation in single/shared bedrooms in family home

Cost £90 bed & breakfast, £95 half board, £100 full board, per week

Insurance not provided

IRELAND

Morrissey Linguistic Centre Ltd   Valhall, Killinure, Athlone, County Westmeath, Ireland

Athlone (353 902) 85160   Fax (353 902) 7821/2

A commercial organisation founded in 1969 organising language courses, homestays, farmstays, riding programmes, golf and sailing programmes

Homestays and farmstays arranged in Athlone, Longford, Roscommon, Birr, Moate, Tipperary and Ballinasloe. Homestays 3/4 weeks, farmstays 3/4/6 weeks.

Individuals and groups

Ages 9-18

Knowledge of English not essential. 15 hours English tuition provided per week. A limited number of places are available for foreign students wishing to attend primary or secondary school for a term or a year.

Weekly coach excursions; full sports facilities and programmes

Full board accommodation in family homes and farms

Cost from £115 per week

Escorted travel to and from airport to central meeting point arranged

Insurance not provided

ENGLAND

Offairte UK Ltd Victoria House, Victoria Street, Taunton, Somerset TAI 3JA

Taunton (01823) 334373

A commercial organisation established in 1988 and specialising in education and language travel. Live n' Learn programme aims to immerse students in their target language by accommodating them in their tutor's home or with a selected host family close by.

Participants can study English in Bournemouth, Exeter and Taunton. 2, 3 or 4 weeks, all year. Apply at least 6 weeks in advance.

Individuals only

Ages 15+

Elementary level of English required; not suitable for beginners. 15, 20 or 25 hours language tuition per week.

Students are included in family activities and outings. Additional activities and excursions can be arranged at extra cost.

Full board accommodation in tutor's home. Single bedroom. All tutors are interviewed in their homes, which are inspected by the Director of Studies or a local representative.

Cost for 2 weeks from £830 (15 hours per week, winter season) to £1,160 (25 hours per week, summer season). All course materials and tourist information provided.

Participants arrange and pay for own travel. Ages 15-16 are met at the airport and accompanied to tutor's home. Adults are met at local coach/rail station by tutor or local representative.

Insurance not provided

ENGLAND, IRELAND, SCOTLAND, WALES

Oxford Accent 2 Bennett Road, Faringdon, Oxfordshire SN7 7AY

Faringdon (01367) 241730

A commercial organisation established in 1976 to provide homestays and holiday language courses

Homestays can be arranged throughout Great Britain and Ireland. 3+ days, all year

Individuals, groups, families and adults

Ages 11+

English language programme available involving 15 hours tuition per week

All types of activities and excursions can be organised on request. Host families may arrange excursions.

Full board accommodation in host families; single/twin room. Host families are inspected once a year.

Cost from £12.50 per night for basic homestay; £26.50 per night includes language tuition

Participants arrange and pay for own international travel. Transfer arrangements from airport to homestay centre can be made at extra cost.

Public liability insurance cover provided

ENGLAND, SCOTLAND, WALES

Pilgrims Progress Tours 18 Ogle Street, London W1P 7LG

0171-436 2174 Fax 0171-436 2192 *020 7*

A commercial organisation established in 1963 as an incoming tour operator for Britain

Homestays arranged in Bournemouth, Chester, London, Torquay, Edinburgh and Cardiff. 3+ days, all year.

Individuals, groups, families and adults

No age limits, but children under 16 must be accompanied

Previous knowledge of English not essential

Local tours can be arranged if booked in advance

Bed and breakfast in family homes, all of which have been inspected

Cost from £12 per person per night. £2 per night supplement for all bookings during June-August.

No insurance provided

Also arrange go-as-you-please bed & breakfast tours; farmstays in the West Country and Scotland

H

ENGLAND, SCOTLAND, WALES

SEE Europe Ltd Inbound Division, 1 Church Walk Studios, Beales Lane, Weybridge, Surrey KT13 8JS

Weybridge (01932) 820216   Fax (01932) 820315

A private organisation set up in 1974 to add an extra dimension to language learning by promoting homestays as a way of experiencing and understanding other peoples' lifestyles and culture

Homestays arranged in London, Surrey, Oxford, Cambridge, Banbury, Cheltenham, Exeter, York, Falmouth, Weston-super-Mare, Ringwood, Rochester, Edinburgh, Stirling, Aberdeen, Holyhead and Llandudno.
4+ nights, all year.

Individuals and groups

Ages 10+

Basic knowledge of English required. Language courses can be arranged for all levels and ages.

Coach excursions arranged to places of interest. Sports/activity programmes also available. Variety of specialised programmes arranged to suit requirements, eg covering agriculture, ecology, aspects of English literature, British theatre or the legal system.

Full board accommodation in family home, with packed lunch on excursion days. Single/twin rooms. Usually 2 students per family.

Cost from £123 per person for 6 nights includes accommodation, entrance fees and activities. Cost varies according to destination, duration, activities and group size. Free places 1:10 for group leaders.

Help can be given with travel arrangements. Meet and greet service available.

H   ABTA FIYTO SAGTA

ENGLAND, SCOTLAND, WALES, IRELAND

Visit Britain 11 The Croft, Hastings, East Sussex TN34 3HH

Hastings (01424) 431438 Fax (01424) 431438

A commercial organisation founded in 1984 offering holidays, homestays, farmstays and courses

Homestays arranged throughout England, Scotland, Wales and Ireland; mainly south east England for young visitors. Any length of stay, all year.

Individuals, groups, families and adults

Ages 12-80

A little English is helpful. Individual tuition available.

Local outings and sports can often be arranged. Most hosts can provide transport and a guide service to places of interest.

Accommodation in carefully selected families, often with teenage children. Each homestay is made on a personal basis, matching the requirements of visitors with the host families.

Cost from £85 half board, £185 full board, per week, depending on type of accommodation and facilities. Registration fee £35.

Visitors can be met at ports/airports, with car/rail transport to family

Insurance not provided

H

Imagine learning French on the Côte d'Azur, with afternoons of windsurfing on the Mediterranean. Or learning Spanish in a remote mountain village in the Sierra Nevada, horse riding at weekends. Study German in the Black Forest or the Austrian Tyrol and improve your folk singing. Sample Italian wines and cooking, or combine language study with painting or pottery in Florence.

Months to go before your A levels, yet you're having problems with your French. You sit on the terrace with a *cappucino* watching the world go by, but dread using your hesitant Italian to order again. You know that mastering German may improve your career propsects but find the evening classes tedious. **STUDY HOLIDAYS** has hundreds of courses to solve your language learning problems.

The Central Bureau's comprehensive guide to European language courses, **STUDY HOLIDAYS** lists hundreds of courses, at all levels from beginner through to advanced or specialist, organised by state or private schools, colleges and universities. **STUDY HOLIDAYS** includes courses in virtually all the European languages. You can brush up on language skills in preparation for examinations, study the language of a country to discover its culture and traditions, or simply learn for enjoyment. Full information is given on each course, including levels, hours of tuition, resources such as language laboratories, accommodation, social activities, and full details of costs. Details are given on courses in support of GCSE or A levels, or where they can lead to recognised examinations or the school's own qualifications.

The courses detailed in **STUDY HOLIDAYS** include opportunities for intensive language learning as well as courses where study is combined with participation in history, civilisation, art, crafts or sports tuition, or simply leisure activities.

The guide also gives information on insurance and health requirements, and where possible gives details of language representatives in the UK where applications can be made for courses abroad. In some cases a full holiday package can be arranged, which can include course fees, accommodation, travel and insurance.

STUDY HOLIDAYS also carries a range of other useful details: sources of grants, scholarships and bursaries; resources, including publications, videos, TV and radio language programmes, services offered by cultural institutes, and other language learning materials.

STUDY HOLIDAYS has opportunities for those aged 6+; from 1 week to 1 year; from Basque to Welsh, French to Spanish, English to Greek; in countries from Austria to Turkey. For further information on the Bureau's publications and programmes contact the Information Desk on © 0171-725 9402.

STUDY HOLIDAYS is published biannually   Seventeenth edition   ISBN 0 900087 90 0   £8.99

UNITED STATES

American Heritage Association   Marylhurst College Campus,
PO Box 147, Marylhurst, Oregon 97036, United States

(1 503) 635-3702   Fax (1 503) 635-8751

A non-profitmaking organisation established in 1957 with a mission to promote educational experiences that encourage an understanding and appreciation of one's own culture and the culture and heritage of others

Homestays arranged in Portland, Seattle and the San Francisco Bay Area. Length of stay depends on needs of group; generally 2-4 weeks, summer, also semester-long college-level programmes.

Groups only, college students and teachers

Ages 16+

Language tuition can be provided

Courses can be arranged to meet the requirements of the group; excursions, field trips and social activities also organised

Full board single/twin room in volunteer host families. Students are treated as part of the family and expected to participate in day-to-day activities.

Costs vary according to type and length of programme

Travel is the responsibility of the group organiser

Insurance can be provided

Also arrange reciprocal exchanges for groups, language study programmes, study programmes at Portland State University, and American adventure programmes

H

UNITED STATES

BASEC (British American Soccer Exchange Club/British American Schools Exchange Club) Kevin Shannon Travel Ltd, 38 Shepherds Bush Road, London W6 7PJ

0181-602 1390

A commercial organisation founded in 1974 to promote cultural visits and exchanges for school parties, giving them the opportunity to experience life in a foreign country. America at Home holidays offer opportunities to live with American families, taking a look at the social, economic and political influences in the US, and to enjoy everyday American life.

Homestays in Florida, California and on the East Coast. 2/3 weeks, Easter and summer.

Groups only (minimum 25 with teacher leader)

Ages 13-17

Cultural programme of activities during the week with sightseeing and visits to schools; weekends spent with host family

Full board accommodation with volunteer host families

Cost £800-£950 per person inclusive of travel, insurance and cultural programme

All travel arrangements made

Insurance included

UNITED STATES

California Experience 35 City Hall Avenue, San Anselmo, California 94960, United States

(1 415) 459 1800   Fax (1 415) 459 6699

A private organisation established in 1992 to provide homestay opportunities for international visitors to California

Homestays arranged in Marin County, California, just north of San Francisco and south of the Napa Valley wine region. 2-4 weeks, all year; longer stays can be arranged. Completed booking forms, including fee, photo and letter of introduction, should be received at least 4 weeks in advance.

Individuals, couples, groups and adults

Ages 16+

Participants should have at least some knowledge of English. Intensive English courses (18 hours per week) can be included in programme.

Can be combined with 20 hours per week voluntary work at the California Center for Wildlife, or with 3-14 day adventure tours of California. Outings may be arranged by host family or representative.

Half board accommodation in family home, with full board at weekends. Single/shared bedroom. Host families are interviewed in their homes and carefully selected on the basis of their interest in hosting visitors, character, and proximity to public transport.

Cost from $500-$1,298, depending on length of stay and whether English course, volunteering or adventure tour programme is included

Participants arrange own international travel. Advice given on bus transfer from San Francisco International Airport; participants met at bus terminal by host family. Representative can meet participants at airport for $95 extra fee. Travel information and maps provided.

Insurance not provided, but participants must have made own arrangements

UNITED STATES

Center for Cultural Interchange (CCI) 42 W 273 Retreat Ct, St Charles, IL 60175, United States

(1 708) 377 2272

Established in 1985, a non profitmaking organisation dedicated to the promotion of cultural understanding, academic development and world peace. Aims to promote a better world through increased cooperation and understanding between individuals, cultures and nations.

Homestays are arranged on the East Coast (New Jersey, Vermont, Connecticut, Pennsylvania, Maryland), the West Coast (California, Oregon, Utah, Washington), the Central States (Iowa, Illinois, Indiana, Wisconsin, Michigan, Ohio, Colorado) and in the South (Florida, Louisiana, Texas). 4-6 weeks, all year. Care is taken to match families with students who are truly compatible in lifestyle and interests.

Individuals or groups

Ages 16-20, individuals; ages 14-19, groups

Students should have a good knowledge of English. Group homestay programme includes 12 hours per week English language tuition.

Group programme includes excursions, activities and social events. Activities can be arranged for individuals at a cost of $50 per week.

Full board accommodation with host family; single/shared room. Potential host families are visited and screened by representatives; references are required and checked. Orientation provided on arrival; students also have the support of a representative at all times.

Individual programme: $200 per week; group programme: from $800 for 4 weeks

Transfers to and from nearest airport are included in the price

Complete accident and medical insurance included

Also arrange programmes in Spain for US students

INDONESIA

Center for Indonesian Studies N70 W237 30 Oakcrest Lane, Sussex, Wisconsin 53089, United States

A non-profit organisation established in 1993 to organise eco-development and cross-cultural study programmes in Indonesia. Has local offices in Bali and Lombok.

Homestay study programmes arranged in the Munduk area of Bali and in the Mataram and Senaru areas of Lombok. 10 weeks, September-December (Lombok) or 15 weeks, February-May (Bali). Apply by 15 October for Bali programme or by 1 May for Lombok programme.

Individuals only

Ages generally 21+. Programmes are designed for undergraduate or postgraduate students of good academic standing, or independent learners educated to degree level.

Knowledge of Indonesian language not required. Substantial language training given 4 times a week, emphasising oral expression and listening comprehension, plus basic reading and writing.

Students attend seminars and take part in weekly field trips outlining aspects of Indonesian history and culture. They also collaborate in small-scale projects with indigenous village communities, organised by Indonesian non-governmental organisations. These may include developing alternative environmental technologies in the villages and eco-cultural tourism in a national park.

Half-board accommodation in Indonesian village families; single rooms

Programme fee $4,500 (10 weeks) or $5,700 (15 weeks)

Participants arrange own travel to Indonesian office. During the programme, transport is laid on.

No insurance provided

H (B D)

CANADA, UNITED STATES

Cultural Homestay International 104 Butterfield Road, San Anselmo, California 94960, United States

(1 415) 459 5397   Fax (1 415) 459 2182

A non-profitmaking organisation set up in 1980 to provide educational programmes for young people and to encourage the growth of friendship and understanding among the peoples of the world

Homestays in all areas of Canada and the United States. Usually 3 weeks, June-August for students; all year round for adults.

Individuals, groups, families and adults

Ages 13+

Knowledge of English not essential. Language classes arranged.

Activities and excursions organised 4 days per week, including study of arts, history and culture, walking tours, visits to museums and local places of interest. Weekends spent with host family.

Half-board single/shared room accommodation in family home. Packed lunch provided if necessary.

Cost $550 for 3 weeks

Insurance not provided

Also arrange homestays in Australia, Canada, China, England, France, Germany, Japan, Mexico, Russia, Slovakia and Spain for North American students and adults

H accommodated wherever possible

UNITED STATES

Educational Resource Development Trust 475 Washington Boulevard, Suite 220, Marina del Rey, California 90292, United States

(I 310) 821 9977   Fax (I 310) 821 9282

A non-profit educational foundation established in 1974 with the goal of providing opportunities for people of different countries to come together and learn about different points of view and ways of life.

Homestays arranged throughout the US, mainly in suburban areas. Usually I month, all year. Also farm/ranchstays for those with some knowledge of rural life; 4-8 weeks, all year. Short-Term Group Study (STGS) programme available for groups during school vacations. Apply at least 8 weeks in advance.

Local representative matches host families and students on the basis of background and interests

Individuals, groups and adults

Ages I5-25+ (special arrangements made for older participants)

Basic conversational English required. STGS programme includes 10-15 hours per week English instruction.

Excursions and activities arranged at discretion of host family. STGS programme includes organised activities and visits.

Full board accommodation in host family; single/shared room. Host families are interviewed in their homes with all family members present, and are required to submit references. Local representative provides support for host family and student for the duration of the stay.

Cost $650-$900 for homestay and farm/ranchstay programmes; $550-$1,250 for STGS programme. Travel and insurance not included.

Individuals make their own travel arrangements. Participants are met at final destination airport by host family and/or local representative. Arrangements can be made to assist young people with airport transfers at major airports, usually at additional cost.

All students must provide proof of adequate medical insurance cover. ERDT offers an insurance package costing approx $40 per month.

H

JAPAN

Exchange: Japan 2120 Packard, PO Box 1166, Ann Arbor, Michigan 48106, United States

(1 313) 665 1820

A non-profit institution established in 1986, committed to the promotion of mutual understanding and global exchange built on excellence in Japanese language training

Exchange: Japan, 1-10-14-501 Minami Aoyama, Manato-ku, Tokyo 107, Japan

Homestays arranged in Kyoto; also in Gujo-Hachiman and Gujo-Shirotori, both in Gifu Prefecture. 7½ weeks, mid June-early August. Apply by early March.

All matching is done at local level by the Japanese administrators familiar with host families. Applicants provide details to help with placement.

Individuals only

Ages 18+

Some knowledge of Japanese necessary, at least one year's study. Programme involves 4 hours Japanese study per day, including speaking, listening, reading and writing.

Weekly programme of activities may include university lectures and a variety of introductions to the culture, such as participation in local festivals, classes in Japanese arts or special events. Extensive opportunity for participants to learn about the community and establish friendships with local people.

Half board accommodation in family home, usually in separate room

Cost $3,760 covers participation fee, tuition, host family honorarium and daily travel to class

Participants make own travel arrangements, but can be met on arrival

Insurance not provided, but all participants must have health insurance cover

AFRICA, ASIA, AUSTRALASIA, THE AMERICAS, MIDDLE EAST

The Experiment in International Living Otesaga, West Malvern Road, Malvern, Worcestershire WR14 4EN

Malvern (01684) 562577

A non-profitmaking educational travel organisation founded in 1936 with the aim of promoting understanding, friendship and respect between people from different cultural backgrounds. Over 40 offices worldwide; details from UK office.

Homestays arranged in Nigeria; Hong Kong, India, Japan, Korea, Malaysia, Nepal, Philippines, Singapore, Thailand; Australia, New Zealand, Polynesia; Canada, Hawaii, Mexico, United States; Argentina, Brazil, Chile, Ecuador, Uruguay; and Israel. 1-4 weeks, all year. Apply 8-10 weeks in advance.

Individuals, families, groups and adults

Ages 16+

Knowledge of the language not necessary. Language courses can be arranged.

Activities and excursions included in group programmes. Professional courses arranged on request.

Full board accommodation in family home varies from single room to floor space, depending on country and family. Families are carefully selected with the understanding that the aim is to allow individuals to experience a different way of life; the circumstances and beliefs of the host family may therefore differ from those of the participants.

Costs vary, depending on country; usually £200-£400, travel extra. Occasional grant aid available on some programmes.

Group travel arrangements can be made; arrangements for individuals on request. Host families will meet participants if requested.

Insurance can be arranged

Also arrange special interest programmes, UK/US high school programmes, US university placement service

UNITED STATES

GIJK Lingua International   Ubierstraße 94, 53173 Bonn, Germany

(49 228) 957300   Fax (49 228) 9573040

A limited company founded in 1983, arranging a variety of international opportunities for young people

Homestays arranged in Connecticut, New York, Massachusetts, Florida, California, Oregon, Washington, Colorado, Minnesota, Alabama, Montana and New Mexico. Also stays on farms and ranches in Colorado. 2-8 weeks, all year.

Individuals only

Ages 16-22 or 14-23 for farm and ranch programme; separate programmes available for ages 22+

Some knowledge of English desirable

Full board accommodation in family home. Families volunteer to take guests and are not paid.

Cost DM1,200 (2 weeks) to DM1,990 (8 weeks)

Help and advice can be given with travel arrangements. Transfers to and from airports arranged.

Insurance not included, but can be provided

Also offer summer schools and courses; au pair stays worldwide

ARGENTINA, AUSTRALIA, BRAZIL, CANADA, CHILE, COSTA RICA, ISRAEL, JAPAN, KOREA, MEXICO, NEW ZEALAND, TAIWAN, VENEZUELA, UNITED STATES

Home Language International Reservations Office, 17 Royal Crescent, Ramsgate, Kent CT11 9PE

Thanet (01843) 851116   Fax (01843) 590300

A commercial organisation set up in 1989, organising immersion language courses where students live with, and are taught by their own private teacher

Participants can study English in Australia, Canada, New Zealand and the United States; Spanish in Argentina, Chile, Costa Rica, Mexico and Venezuela; Portuguese in Brazil, Hebrew in Israel, Japanese in Japan, Korean in Korea and Chinese in Taiwan. I+ weeks, all year. Apply I month in advance (2 months for the Far East and South America).

Individuals, adults and children

Ages 8+

No previous knowledge of language necessary. Usually 15, 20 or 25 hours language tuition per week.

Excursions and other activities can be provided, but usually at extra cost where, for example, entrance fees are involved

Full board accommodation in teacher's family home. Shared programme available where two students wish to learn together. Every effort made to match teacher's interests with those of the student. Organisers visit potential teachers to verify that home is suitable and qualifications genuine, and will also contact students to monitor progress.

Costs vary according to intensity of tuition. For example, I week in the US from $800 (15 hours tuition, shared) to $1,250 (25 hours, 1:1).

Transfers can be arranged to and from teacher's home at extra cost

Insurance not provided

Also offer, on the same basis, business and specialised vocabulary courses, and 5 star luxury specialised courses

H

ARGENTINA, AUSTRALIA, BRAZIL, CANADA, COSTA RICA, JAPAN, MEXICO, TAIWAN, UNITED STATES

International Language Homestays 2 Cecil Square, Margate, Kent CT9 1BD

Thanet (01843) 227700   Fax (01843) 223377

A commercial organisation set up in 1989 organising immersion language courses where individual students live with, and are taught by their own private teacher

Participants can learn Spanish in Argentina, Costa Rica and Mexico; English in Australia, Canada, and the United States; French in Canada; Portuguese in Brazil; Mandarin Chinese in Taiwan; and Japanese in Japan. 1+ weeks, all year.

Individuals, families and adults

All ages

Each course is tailor-made for the individual with 15, 20 or 25 hours language tuition per week

Students are fully integrated into the social life and activities of the family. Living with the language teacher means students are guided and corrected not only during lessons but also when accompanying the teacher on family activities and excursions. If sufficient notice is given students can be placed with teachers who share their special interests.

Full board accommodation in teacher's family home. A sharing programme is available if two participants wish to book together.

Costs vary according to location and tuition; private tuition and full board accommodation from £370 per week

Transfers can be arranged to and from host teacher's home at extra cost

Insurance not provided

JAPAN

International Links 145 Manygate Lane, Shepperton, Middlesex TW17 9EP

Walton-on-Thames (01932) 229300   Fax (01932) 222294

A commercial organisation set up in 1988 to promote language learning through homestays

Homestays arranged in Ise City and Osaka. 2-4 weeks, all year.

Individuals only

No age limits; depends on individual requirements

Applicants should have some interest in either Japanese language or culture. Language tuition can be arranged at £18 per hour.

Excursions to places of interest can be arranged

Full board accommodation. Single room in family home. Families are visited to ensure high standards.

Cost approx £200 per week

Transfers can be arranged at extra cost

Insurance can be provided

H

INDIA, NEPAL

Munjeeta Travel 12 Cavendish Road, Woking, Surrey GU22 0EP

Woking (01483) 773331

A private company established in 1987 to promote friendship between people from West and East, specialising in designing tailor-made holiday programmes to India with accommodation in local host families

Homestays arranged throughout India and Nepal; plans to extend into Burma. 2+ weeks, all year, depending on individual requirements. Apply at least 3 months in advance; proprietor prefers to meet people individually in order to discuss their requirements.

Individuals, families and adults

No age limiits

Knowledge of foreign languages not necessary

Tours and activities can be arranged to suit individual requirements. Host may act as sightseeing guide.

Full board accommodation in family home. All families are carefully selected for their warmth and hospitality.

Cost varies from £800 upwards, including return fare on British Airways, travel within host country, sightseeing and accommodation

Guests are met by host on arrival, and seen off by host on departure

Travel insurance can be arranged

H experience in dealing with physically disabled/wheelchairs

AFRICA, ASIA, THE AMERICAS, AUSTRALASIA, EUROPE

Servas General Secretary, Vibeke Matorp, Birkedals Alle 40, Fruens Boge, 5250 Odense SV, Denmark

(45) 66 17 02 40

Established in 1949, a non-profit, non-governmental, inter-racial and international association of hosts and travellers which works towards understanding, peace and justice through person-to-person contacts

Servas UK, Hazel Barham, 41 Pendre, Brecon, Powys LD3 9EA
℗ Brecon (01874) 622672   Fax (01874) 625694

Represented in nearly every country, with over 13,000 hosts worldwide. Hosts offer to provide a bed for 2 nights (or longer by invitation).

Individuals only

Ages 18+. All travellers are interviewed to make sure they are responsible and open minded. Each traveller then receives a letter of introduction, valid for one year, which is shown on arrival in a host's home. Potential travellers should join in plenty of time, allowing at least 4 weeks before departure to contact the hosts they wish to visit.

English is the official language; no specific language knowledge is necessary, just the ability and desire to communicate with hosts

Activities are entirely at the discretion of the host

Accommodation provided varies depending on host; most will provide a bed and invite the traveller to share an evening meal. Those unable to provide overnight accommodation may act as day hosts, prepared to meet the traveller for a meal, a chat, a workplace visit or guided tour.

Costs vary according to country. Hosts are volunteers and do not charge for accommodation. To obtain a copy of a country's host list, travellers pay a deposit, refundable when the list is returned at the end of the trip together with a short report.

Travel is the responsibility of the individual traveller. Hosts are not obliged to meet travellers on arrival, nor to provide transport for them.

Insurance not provided

H Hosts specify in their listing if they can cater for disabled travellers

NEPAL

Universal Correspondence Organisation of Nepal Bansbari, PO Box 1571, Kathmandu, Nepal

(977 1) 410758

A private organisation set up in 1979 to promote international peace and understanding through correspondence, exchange and home visits

Homestays arranged in the towns of Kathmandu, Bharatpur, Biratnagar and in the country areas of Nawalpur and Harion. 2+ days, all year.

Individuals only

Ages 18-60

Good knowledge of English required

Visitors are taken to local group meetings, fairs, the theatre and family ceremonies such as weddings and other parties. Arrangements can also be made to talk to Nepalese people over a meal, without the offer of accommodation.

Accommodation in typical Nepalese home. European breakfast and two Nepalese-style meals (rice, dal, vegetables) provided per day. Guests should take a sleeping bag.

Costs are settled according to facilities required by guest

Guests can be met at Tribhuvan International Airport, Kathmandu by prior arrangement

Insurance not provided

FIOCES

BRAZIL

Ventura Viagens Estudantis Rua do Catete 311, Sala 407, CEP 222220 Rio de Janeiro, Brazil

(55 21) 265 0248   Fax (55 21) 205 8191

A student travel agency arranging homestays in Brazil

Homestays arranged in Copacabana, Ipanema and Flamengo. 1+ weeks, all year.

Individuals and and groups

No age limits

Knowledge of Portuguese an advantage

Activities arranged

Bed and breakfast accommodation in family home

Cost US$10-US$17 per person per night

Insurance not provided

CANADA, UNITED STATES

World Exchange White Birch Road, Putnam Valley, New York 10579, United States

(1 914) 526 2505   Fax (1 914) 528 9187

A non-profitmaking organisation founded in 1985 and specialising in arranging homestays in Canada and the US. Host families are unpaid and participate with the aim of developing international friendships.

Homestays arranged in Ontario and New York, Massachusetts, New Jersey, Pennsylvania, Maryland, Virginia, Florida, the Mid-West and California. 2-4 weeks, all year.

Individuals and groups

Ages 13-25

Minimum 2 years' study of English required. Language tuition can be arranged.

One full-day trip arranged, plus farewell party organised by local programme director

Full board accommodation in family home. Host families are carefully selected and interviewed to ensure suitability. Head office and local staff offer continuous support and assistance.

Cost $550-$850, excluding travel, depending on area and length of stay

Guests are met at nearest airport by host family or director

Insurance not provided. Participants must take out their own medical insurance.

All the essential advice and information you need to arrange a successful and enjoyable seasonal job is in the Central Bureau's information guide **WORKING HOLIDAYS**, acknowledged as *the* authoritative guide.

WORKING HOLIDAYS lists hundreds of employers offering over 99,000 temporary or seasonal jobs in Britain and 70 other countries. Whatever the job, in whatever country, **WORKING HOLIDAYS** gives very full details. Any age or nationality restrictions are noted, the period of work on offer, salary and terms, including whether travel, accommodation or insurance is included is listed, and application deadlines are given. But it doesn't stop there.

WORKING HOLIDAYS carries information on a wide range of other useful details: where and how to advertise for a job in a foreign newspaper, services of local youth information centres, useful publications to help you plan your visit, what work or residence permit you'll need and how to go about getting it, what medical precautions you should take, what insurance cover you should have, and what passports or visas will get you across borders. It lists addresses and telephone numbers of embassies, high

From picking pears in Australia to being an au pair in Greece; from excavating Inca remains in South America to restoring medieval castles in France; from teaching sports in the USA to cooking in Switzerland, **WORKING HOLIDAYS** has thousands of opportunities and a wealth of information to help you see the world.

commissions, youth and student travel offices, youth hostels, passport and tourist offices and other organisations to help you, tells you all about accommodation, insurance, health requirements, money and travel, and provides just about everything else you'll need not only to get a holiday job but to make the whole experience as fulfilling and trouble-free as possible.

Unlike some other guides, every piece of information in **WORKING HOLIDAYS** is checked each and every year, and updated against reports and other received information. Combine this with the latest in information technology we use to edit and produce the guide and you can be sure that the information you will be using to choose your holiday is right up to date.

WORKING HOLIDAYS has opportunities for those aged 12-70+, younger if accompanied; from 3 days up to a year; from Au pairs to Zoo staff; from Austria to Zimbabwe. It is available from all good bookshops or direct form the Central Bureau. For further information on the Bureau's publications and programmes contact the Information Desk on ✆ 0171-725 9402.

WORKING HOLIDAYS is published each November for the following year.

ENGLAND : BELGIUM, FRANCE, SWITZERLAND

Alphalingua 1A Aveley Lane, Farnham, Surrey GU9 8PN

Farnham (01252) 725118

A private company established in 1988 to enable and encourage English and French-speaking students to take part in exchanges and learn about one another's language and culture

Exchanges arranged between England (London, Surrey, Hampshire) and Belgium/France/Switzerland. 10 days-3 weeks, during school holidays.

Parents fill in a questionnaire with details of student and family, including interests and sports. The student is interviewed in his/her home and paired with a French-speaking student with regard to age, background, interests and personality. To have a better chance of a good match, apply in September for the following summer,

Individuals only

Ages 12-18

At least a basic knowledge of relevant language required

Participants share in family activities, including any trips the family may arrange

Full board accommodation in family home; single/shared room

Cost £10 registration fee, plus £20 contact fee

Participants make own travel arrangements; hosts meet guests on arrival

Insurance not provided

Also arrange term stays in English boarding schools and summer visits to adventure camps for French children; French courses and summer camps for English children

H

BRITAIN / IRELAND : FRANCE

Amitié Internationale des Jeunes 36 Chaulden House Gardens, Hemel Hempstead, Hertfordshire HP1 2BW

Hemel Hempstead (01442) 250886

A private commercial organisation founded in 1947 aiming to promote friendships between young people and their families and the improvement of language skills

Amitié Internationale des Jeunes, 33 avenue d'Eylau, 75116 Paris, France ✆ (33 1) 47 27 75 64

Exchanges arranged throughout Britain, Ireland and France. 2 weeks, Easter and summer. Each child receives/visits during a holiday period, and visits/receives during the following vacation; during the summer the visits are immediately consecutive. The holiday may not always be spent in the family's permanent town of residence. School reference and medical certificate required.

Applications are dealt with individually, and applicants with similar ages and background are carefully matched

Individuals only

Ages 10-18/19

One year's knowledge of French/English required

Families outline activities envisaged on the application form

Full board accommodation in single/shared bedrooms

Cost from £195-£240 covers insurance, agency fees and return travel London/Paris

Escorted travel by boat/train or air to Paris/London, where participants are met by host families

Medical and personal liability insurance provided

BRITAIN : AUSTRIA

Anglo-Austrian Society 46 Queen Anne's Gate, London SW1H 9AU

0171-222 0366

A non-profitmaking charity founded in 1944 to promote educational and cultural exchange between Britain and Austria

Anglo-Austrian Society, Stubenring 24, 1010 Vienna, Austria
© (43 1) 512 98 03/4

Exchanges arranged throughout Britain and Austria. 2/3/4 weeks, Easter and summer.

Applicants are carefully selected and matched according to age, hobbies, interests and schooling. References are taken up and first consideration is given to choosing the right partner. Exchanges can be arranged over 2 years, but usually only for younger applicants.

Individuals and groups

Ages 13-17

Some knowledge of German/English helpful, but not essential

Visitors are included in all family outings and activities

Full board accommodation in single/shared bedrooms

Cost £250 inclusive; some £120 travel bursaries available

Escorted parties by arrangement from all parts of Britain to all parts of Austria; participants are then personally introduced to the respective families

Insurance provided

Also offer language courses and special interest holidays

BRITAIN : ITALY

Anglo-Italian Holidays 44 Kyrle Road, London SW11 6BA

0171-978 4926

A private organisation set up in 1985 to help young Italians and Britons visit each other's country and sample each other's way of life

Exchanges arranged between Britain and Italy. Regions in Italy are mainly Tuscany and the areas around Genoa, Venice and Milan.

Participants are matched according to age, background, interests and personality. Great care and attention is given to matching each individual student.

Individuals and adults

Ages 15+

Previous knowledge of Italian/English not necessary

Families arrange excursions and entertainments

Full board accommodation in family homes. Single room, or shared with exchange partner.

Registration fee £90; no accommodation charge

Participants are met at airport by host family

Insurance not provided

Also arrange au pair stays in Italy and England

BRITAIN : FRANCE, GERMANY, SPAIN

Dragons International The Old Vicarage, South Newington, Banbury, Oxfordshire OX15 4JN

Banbury (01295) 721717   Fax (01295) 721991

A commercial organisation founded in 1975 and specialising in individual exchanges and homestays

Dragons International, 16 rue de la Chapelle, 78630 Orgeval, France ✆ (33) 39 75 53 40

Dragons International, Sra Reyes Tornero Castanon, Apartado de Correos 239, Torrejon de Ardoz, 28850 Madrid ✆ (34 1) 676 7342

Exchanges arranged between all parts of Britain, France, Germany and Spain. 2 weeks, March-August.

Applicants are carefully matched with a partner of their own age, interests and home background

Individuals and groups

Ages 11-19

Basic knowledge of the relevant language required

Host families arrange outings

Full board accommodation in single/shared rooms.

Britain and France: £169-£199 depending on point of departure, covers return travel, administrative costs and insurance. Germany and Spain: £95 fee includes insurance.

Britain/France: supervised coach transport from 17 points in Britain, 11 points in France. Britain/Spain, Germany: travel arranged privately.

Fully comprehensive insurance provided

UNOSEL

BRITAIN : FRANCE

Euro Teenage Exchange/ETE Hillyfields House, Hillyfields, Sidcot, Winscombe, Avon BS25 1PH

Winscombe (01934) 842690   Fax (01934) 843248

A private organisation established in March 1994 to offer a Teenage Life Register, a personalised exchange system between English and French teenagers, enabling them to develop one or several relationships over the time that they themselves need before the exchange takes place, thus allowing for greater confidence in finding a friend for life and forging lasting links between the two families

ETE, Domaine de la Tyre, 65700 Castlenau Rivière Basse, Hautes Pyrénées, France

Families themselves decide on the time of the exchange, length of stay and all travel arrangements

Applicants are matched on the basis of a detailed questionnaire. Registration and fee guarantees families a place on the database for up to 9 years. Annual updates are made to cover any change in circumstances.

Individuals only

Ages 11-19

Proficiency in French/English not essential; applicants are matched according to language ability

Families are encouraged to organise activities for their exchange visitor

Exchange visitors are welcomed into the family home and treated as a family member. Single/shared room.

Sliding scale of fees according to age: from £60 for registration, from £25 when a suitable match is made. If a satisfactory exchange family has not been found within 12 months, the registration fee is refunded.

Families make their own travel arrangements

Families are advised to arrange suitable insurance cover

BRITAIN, IRELAND : FRANCE

Maison de Cambridge British Cultural Centre, I rue Général Riu, 34000 Montpellier, France

(33) 67 64 07 86   Fax (33) 67 64 73 94

The British Cultural Centre, registered under French associations and charities legislation, was founded in 1977. Renamed Maison de Cambridge in 1984, when a joint committee of teachers and others from the education authorities in Cambridge and Montpellier organised a community link.

Summer holiday exchanges arranged between France (mainly the south) and Britain and the Republic of Ireland. Participants spend 6 weeks with their partners, 3 weeks in France and 3 weeks in the British Isles. Both exchange visits usually take place in the same year.

Partners are matched essentially on the basis of age and interests

Individuals only

Ages 13-18 (approx)

At least one year of French/English necessary

All activities during the stay are arranged by participants' families

Accommodation with partner's family, usually in separate bedrooms

Cost £400-£500 depending on departure and destination airports, dates of travel, and whether individual or group travel. Cost includes air travel, transfers, overnight costs, insurance, overheads and escort service. Pocket money not included. Escorts remain in attendance throughout the exchange.

Full travel and cancellation insurance included

BRITAIN : FORMER SOVIET UNION

Society for Cooperation in Russian and Soviet Studies
320 Brixton Road, London SW9 6AB

0171-274 2282

A charity founded in 1924 to promote the exchange of language and culture between Britain and what was then the USSR through individual contacts at all levels

Russian Association for International Cooperation and Development, 14 Vozdvizhenka Street, Moscow 103885, Russia

Exchanges arranged between Britain and the Former Soviet Union (FSU). Up to 3 weeks, all year.

Individuals, groups and adults

Ages 14+

Some previous knowledge of the language helpful but not essential. All tours have Russian/English-speaking guides. Language tuition provided for some groups.

Visits to places of interest arranged. Host family arranges evening outings.

Half board accommodation in family home; single/shared bedrooms

Non-currency exchanges; each side pays their own fare to host country and is treated as guest from point of arrival

Participants travel in a group, with a guide in charge

Insurance provided

Also offer extensive resource centre and library on the FSU and pre-revolutionary Russia. Associated charity can offer small grants for educational visits to the FSU.

A period of voluntary service can be enriching and rewarding, involving volunteers in improving the quality of life and community environment. Opportunities to take on a demanding challenge exist in developed and developing countries, and all the essential advice and information needed to arrange a successful, constructive placement is in the Central Bureau's guide VOLUNTEER WORK, the authoritative guide that has found worthwhile placements for thousands of volunteers.

A quarter of the world's population still lives in poverty; almost a fifth is non-literate; the opening up of Eastern Europe and the need to rebuild economies has revealed another skills shortage which volunteers can help fill. Even in so-called developed countries working to overcome the problems caused by poverty, bad housing and illiteracy, presents a worthwhile challenge. VOLUNTEER WORK offers invaluable information and advice to those considering volunteering.

VOLUNTEER WORK has comprehensive details on volunteer-sending agencies recruiting and placing volunteers for medium and long-term service, from a few months up to several years, in Britain and 120 countries worldwide. Advice is given on selecting an agency and a personal checklist is provided to evaluate potential. Each agency is profiled, giving information on its origins, orientation and philosophy, countries of operation, projects arranged, personal qualities and skills required, length and terms of service, briefing and relevant literature. Practical information and advice includes everything from invaluable insights from development workers and returned volunteers, through preparation and training, advisory bodies, to health, travel and insurance.

Typical projects include assisting in the provision of vocational training in the South Pacific islands; helping run women's literacy classes in rural India; organising nutrition programmes with the Guruani Indians of Bolivia; working with the homeless poor at a creative non-violence community in the US; helping with the resettlement and education of refugees in Britain; and protecting the rights of the disadvantaged to education and representation in France.

VOLUNTEER WORK has opportunities for those aged 16+; from 3 weeks to 3 years; from agricultural projects to town planning schemes; from placements for business advisers to midwives; from Antigua to Western Samoa. For short-term opportunities, the Central Bureau guide WORKING HOLIDAYS provides information on thousands of placements lasting from a long weekend to 3 months. For further information on the Bureau's publications and programmes contact the Information Desk on ✆ 0171-725 9402.

VOLUNTEER WORK is published biannually.   Fifth edition   ISBN 0 900087 92 7   £8.99

THE AMERICAS, ASIA, AUSTRALASIA, EUROPE

AFS Intercultural Education Programmes Ground Floor Suite, Arden House, Wellington Street, Bingley, West Yorkshire BD16 2NB

Bingley (01274) 560677   Fax (01274) 567675

Registered charity, founded in 1947 as a partner of the American organisation AFS Intercultural Programs. Aims to work towards peace through international understanding, promoting relationships in which those from different cultural backgrounds share new learning situations.

Term stays arranged; different countries selected each year. 11 months from July/August or from January/February. Participants may return earlier; this applies especially to those intending to return to higher education in September. Apply preferably before November of year prior to commencement of programme; late applicants occasionally considered. Applicants outside the UK should apply to the organisation cooperating with AFS Intercultural Programs in their home country.

Individuals only

Ages 16-18 (some destinations 16-19). Applicants should be attending school full-time, be in good health, adaptable and willing to give a lot to the experience.

No special language knowledge required. Introductory language course provided on arrival.

Participants attend school full-time and become a member of the community. Group activities, language and cultural orientation courses organised; host families may arrange outings.

Full board accommodation in family home. Applicants are carefully placed in a family and community which complements their background. Families are volunteers and receive no fee for hosting.

Cost from £900-£3,850 includes travel, placement in school and family, accommodation, medical expenses, orientation courses, group activities, and support and supervision throughout the stay. Parents are asked to make a realistic contribution within their means; participants will be encouraged to seek grants from local trusts and companies.

Travel included

Insurance included

UNITED STATES

Center for Cultural Interchange (CCI) 42 W 273 Retreat Ct, St Charles, IL 60175, United States

(1 708) 377 2272

Established in 1985, a non-profitmaking organisation dedicated to the promotion of cultural understanding, academic development and world peace. Aims to promote a better world through increased cooperation and understanding between individuals, cultures and nations.

Term stays arranged throughout the United States. 5 or 10 months. Care is taken to match families with students who are truly compatible in lifestyle and interests. Apply by 15 April.

Individuals only

Ages 15-18. Students are selected on the basis of English language ability, scholastic aptitude, cross-cultural skills and motivation.

Students must be sufficiently proficient in English to understand the material presented to them in the American classroom

Students attend an American high school and take part in school activities. They may also have the opportunity to take part in community service.

Full board accommodation with host family; single/shared room. Potential host families are visited and screened by trained representatives; references are required and checked. A student orientation is provided on arrival; students also have the support of a representative at all times.

Cost $2,350 for 5 months, $2,650 for 10 months

Transfers to and from nearest airport included

Complete accident and medical insurance included

Also arrange programmes in Spain for US students

UNITED STATES

Educational Resource Development Trust's SHARE! High School Exchange Program 475 Washington Boulevard, Suite 220, Marina del Rey, California 90292, United States

(1 310) 821 9977   Fax (1 310) 821 9282

A non-profit educational foundation established in 1974 with the goal of providing opportunities for people of different countries to come together and learn about different points of view and ways of life

Term stays arranged throughout the United States, mainly in suburban areas. 5 months, beginning mid January (apply by 31 October); 5 or 10 months beginning mid August (apply by 1 May).

Local representative matches host families and students on the basis of background and interests

Individuals only

Ages 15-18. Applicants should be of above average academic ability.

Good knowledge of English required; minimum 3 years' study

Participants attend a local high school as a regular student. They should be prepared to make real contributions to their school, community and host family, participating as active members of the household as well as sharing their own country's culture, history and traditions.

Full board accommodation in host family; single/shared room. Prospective host families are interviewed in their homes with all family members present, and are required to submit references. Local representative provides support for host family and student for the duration of the stay.

Cost $2,400-$3,500, not including travel or insurance costs

Individuals make their own travel arrangements, but are met at final destination airport by host family and/or local representative. Arrangements can usually be made to assist with airport transfers, at additional cost.

All students must provide proof that they have adequate medical insurance cover. ERDT offers an insurance package, cost approx $40 per month.

H

FRANCE, BRITAIN / IRELAND

En Famille 38 Longfield Road, Bristol BS7 9AG

Bristol (0117) 942 5779   Fax (0117) 942 5779

A non-profitmaking organisation, established 1978, awaiting registration as a charity. Close working relationship with a similar French organisation, ALLEF. Aims to give English and French children the opportunity to acquaint themselves, in depth, with each other's language and culture.

ALLEF (Apprendre Les Languages En Famille), 18 rue Blanche, 79000 Niort, France   ℗ (33) 49 33 24 70

Term stays arranged on an exchange basis between Britain/Ireland and France. 6 months, each way. One-way visits arranged very occasionally. Ideally information about prospective participants should be received well in advance, so that the exchange can be thoroughly prepared.

Individuals only

Ages 8-11

Knowledge of French/English not essential. Participants will usually begin to speak the other language fluently after 3 months.

The visiting child is treated as a member of the family and takes part in family activities. Permission must also be obtained from the school for the visiting child to attend.

Full board accommodation in family homes. Great care is taken to choose families of similar background and outlook, with child of similar age. Families may make preliminary visits.

Cost £450 inclusive of host school fee and all administrative and monitoring costs. One-way visits cost an additional £90 per month.

H depending on circumstances

ENGLAND

English Schools Study Programme (ESSPRO) 49 Park Road, Woking, Surrey GU22 7BZ

Woking (01483) 727543

A commercial organisation set up in 1987 to allow foreign students to participate in the full English schools system as an alternative to enrolment in purely English language tuition schools

Term stays arranged in both state-run and private schools in south east England. 1+ months, all year; minimum stay of 1 term advised.

Individuals and groups

Ages 8-18

Conversational English necessary. Extra English tuition can be arranged.

Excursions and activities such as tennis or riding arranged on request. Families organise visits to the theatre and outings to London and other places of interest.

Full board accommodation in single room in family home; all homes inspected

Cost £85 per week for accommodation, plus tuition/school fees

Host families will meet guests on arrival

Insurance not provided

FRANCE, GERMANY, SPAIN

European Educational Opportunities Programme 28 Canterbury Road, Lydden, Dover, Kent CT15 7ER

Dover (01304) 830948/823631   Fax (01304) 831914/825869

A non-profitmaking organisation founded in 1986 aiming to offer high-quality programmes through carefully selected homes, schools and allied agencies

Term stays arranged in France (Auxerre), Germany (Cologne, Munich, Bremen, Hanover) and Spain (Madrid, Valladolid, Salamanca). 1+ terms, all year.

Individuals only

Ages 16+

Reasonable fluency in the relevant language essential. Private language tuition can be arranged.

Participants attend local schools and enter fully into academic and social programmes; they must be recommended by their own school

Full board accommodation in family home. Students are totally integrated into the family, and are supported and supervised by a member of staff. Parents may telephone at any time to discuss problems or areas of concern.

Cost from £508 per month

Insurance not provided

H

ENGLAND, WALES, IRELAND, CHANNEL ISLANDS

European Educational Opportunities Programme 28 Canterbury Road, Lydden, Dover, Kent CT15 7ER

Dover (01304) 830948/823631   Fax (01304) 831914/825869

A non-profitmaking organisation founded in 1986 aiming to offer high-quality programmes through carefully selected homes, schools and allied agencies.

Term stays arranged in Surrey, Kent, Essex, East Anglia, West Country, Yorkshire, Channel Islands, Wales and Ireland. 1+ terms, all year.

Individuals only

Ages 16+

Reasonable fluency in English essential. Private English tuition arranged on request.

Participants attend local grammar/high schools and enter fully into academic and social programmes; they must be recommended by their own school

Full board accommodation in family home. Students are totally integrated into the family, and are supported and supervised by a member of staff. Parents may telephone at any time to discuss problems or areas of concern.

Costs from £379 per month, plus £20 registration fee

In certain circumstances group or escorted travel can be arranged

Insurance not provided

H

DENMARK, FINLAND, FRANCE, IRELAND, SWEDEN

GIJK High School International Ubierstraße 94, 53173 Bonn, Germany

(49 228) 957300   Fax (49 228) 9573020

A limited company founded in 1983, arranging a variety of international opportunities

Term stays arranged in Denmark, Finland, France, Ireland and Sweden. 2,7 or 10 months, beginning January, April or September.

Individuals only

Ages 15-18

Good knowledge of relevant language required for stays in France and Ireland

Students attend a local *lycée* or high school and take part in school activities. A local coordinator is on hand throughout the stay to help with any problems that may arise.

Full board accommodation in family home. All families are visited and carefully selected.

Cost varies depending on country, length and dates of stay; for example, France from DM3,390 (2 months) to DM9,890 (10 months)

Help and advice can be given with travel arrangements

Insurance not provided

Also offer summer schools and courses; au pair stays worldwide

AUSTRALIA, UNITED STATES

GIJK High School International Ubierstraße 94, 53173 Bonn, Germany

(49 228) 957300 Fax (49 228) 9573020

A limited company founded in 1983, arranging a variety of international opportunities for young people

Term stays arranged in Australia and the United States. 5 or 10 months, beginning January or August. 3 month programme available in Australia only, beginning January or June.

Individuals only

Ages 15-17 (Australia) or 15-18 (United States)

Good knowledge of English required

Students attend a local school and take part in school activities. Orientation seminars held prior to departure and on arrival. A local coordinator is on hand throughout the stay to help with any problems that may arise.

Full board accommodation in family home

Australia: DM,7950 (3 months) to DM9,850 (10 months).
United States: DM7,940 (5 months) to DM8,940 (10 months).

Return travel from Frankfurt included

Health insurance included in United States programme

Also offer au pair stays worldwide

UNITED STATES

International Student Exchange Inc PO Box 840, Fort Jones, California 96032, United States

(1 916) 468-2264 or toll free within the US (800) 766-4656
Fax (1 916) 486-2060

A non-profitmaking organisation founded in 1982 as a result of requests for an international programme responsive to the needs of students and parents. Through carefully matching foreign teenagers with typical American families, hopes to strengthen world harmony and build lasting friendships.

Term stays arranged in small towns and rural areas throughout the US. 6, 10 or 12 months.

Individuals only

Ages 15-18. Students must complete an extensive application form covering autobiographical details, school report, medical details, letters of recommendation and photographs.

Minimum 2 years' English study required

Student attends high school during stay and participates in all family activities including holidays

Full board accommodation in carefully matched host family, either in separate bedroom or shared with another child in the family

Cost $2,800, 6 months; $2,900, 10 months; $3,900, 12 months

Insurance provided

H

FRANCE, BRITAIN

Maison de Cambridge   British Cultural Centre, 1 rue Général Riu, 34000 Montpellier, France

(33) 67 64 07 86   Fax (33) 67 64 73 94

The British Cultural Centre, registered under French associations and charities legislation, was founded in 1977. Renamed Masion de Cambridge in 1984, when a joint committee of teachers and others from the education authorities in Cambridge and Montpellier organised a community link.

One, two or three-term stays arranged in France (mainly Mediterranean coast and south inland areas) and term exchanges arranged between French-speaking and English-speaking pupils. Term stay participants spend one or more terms in a French school and usually stay in the family of a pupil from the school attended. Term exchange participants spend one half-term with their French partner in France and one half-term with the French partner in the British Isles. They are family to family exchanges and both partners attend the same schools.

Partners are matched on the basis of age, interests, sex and family background

Individuals only

Ages 14+

A minimum of 2 years French/English is necessary

All activities during the stay are organised by participant's family

Accommodation with partner's family, usually in separate bedrooms

Cost £400-£500 includes air travel, transfer between airports, overnight costs, insurance, escort costs and overheads. Pocket money not included.

Full travel and cancellation insurance included

FRANCE, GERMANY, SPAIN

Study Associates International European Division, Gold Peak House, Wilmerhatch Lane, Epsom, Surrey KT18 7EH

Ashtead (01372) 275005   Fax (01372) 273976

Established in 1983, specialises in responsible international student exchange programmes for teenagers student wishing to venture overseas to live and study, often for the first time. Run by British parents and offers year-round support to the students during their time abroad through full-time local staff in each of the countries offered.

Term stays arranged in France, Germany and Spain. 3, 5 or 10 months, beginning January or September. Most applications processed 8-18 months prior to start of programme; limited number accepted up to 4 months prior.

Individuals only

Ages 16-19. Most applicants will be taking a year between school and university. Minimum 5 GCSEs grade C or above; A level desirable, although not essential as study habits, motivation and commitment to the programme are of equal importance. British school recommendation required.

Students who do not have the relevant language at A level may take a preparation course before transferring to the term stay programme

Students attend a *lycée, Gymnasium* or Spanish high school, whilst studying alongside European youngsters of their chosen country

Full board accommodation with carefully selected host family. Students have the year-round support of a community representative in addition to the full-time local staff.

Programme fees from £1,890, 3 months, £2,545, 5 months and £3,145, 10 months

Fees do not include travel arrangements

Medical insurance compulsory; not included in programme fee

UNITED STATES

Study Associates International Academic Year in the USA, Gold Peak House, Wilmerhatch Lane, Epsom, Surrey KT18 7EH

Ashtead (01372) 275005   Fax (01372) 273976

Established in 1983, specialises in responsible international student exchange programmes to the US and Europe, for students wishing to study abroad often for the first time. Run by British parents and offers year-round support prior to departure and during the programme through full-time staff in each of the countries offered.

Term stays arranged throughout the US. 5 months (January-June) or 10 months (August-June). Most applications processed 8-18 months prior to start of programme; limited number accepted up to 4 months prior.

Applicants' personal interests, hobbies, background and personality are considered when finalising a placement

Individuals only

Ages 15-19. Students must have at least 5 GCSEs and are required to provide a British school recommendation.

Students attend an American high school and live with a carefully selected host family. The high schools offer an exciting school curriculum with a broad range of subjects often not available in the UK, including excellent sports, music and drama opportunities.

Full board accommodation in host family. All families are screened prior to selection. Each student also has a local community representative and regional manager, supported by full-time national and regional offices.

Programme fees from £2,545, 5 months and £2,990, 10 months

Roundtrip transatlantic airfare included

Medical insurance compulsory; not included in programme fee

ENGLAND

White House Guardianships 34 Talbot Road, Bournemouth BH9 2JF

Bournemouth (01202) 521100   Fax (01202) 521100

A private organisation established in 1992 to promote education for foreign pupils in the British state and private school sectors. Pupils participate in the school's full curriculum and live with an English family.

Apply through nearest agency; details on request

Term stays arranged at schools in Devon, Dorset, Kent, Yorkshire, Wiltshire and the Isle of Wight. 1+ terms, beginning September or January; students return home for Christmas and Easter holidays. Apply at least 6 months in advance.

All host families are inspected and interviewed at length to ensure their suitability and recognition of responsibilities, and are notified to the local authority's Social Services Department and vetted by them in accordance with the Children Act. Students must submit medical and school references, and undergo English and psychological tests. Every effort made to make placements with families with children of a similar age attending the same school, and with similar interests and character.

Individuals only

Ages 8-18 (private schools) or 11-18 (state schools)

Students should have some knowledge of English learned at school

Students participate in full academic, social and sporting programme of the school and in the life of the host family

Full board accommodation in family home, with lunch at school during the school day. Single room.

Costs include flights and vary depending upon distance and school

All pupils are met on arrival and escorted to family home

Students in education for 6+ months are accepted into the UK National Health Service. Other insurance should be taken out in home country.

Also arrange short stay programmes for groups

UNITED STATES

Youth Exchange Service Inc 4675 MacArthur Court, Suite 830, Newport Beach, California 92660, United States

(1 714) 955 2030   Fax (1 714) 955 0232

A non-profitmaking organisation established in 1974 and composed of a network of voluntary representatives worldwide. The objective is to promote world peace and understanding by immersing students in the language and culture of a foreign country.

Stays are arranged throughout the United States, including all of the major cities. 6/9 months, starting January or August/September.

Individuals only

Ages 15-18

Excellent knowledge of English required. Students must have a reference from their English language teacher, attend formal English classes from recognised institutions and pass an oral and written examination prior to acceptance into the programme. Students must submit three references, pass a health examination and have a good scholastic record.

Students attend a local high school and participate in school life. Local representatives arrange outings to places of interest.

Full board accommodation with volunteer host families. Single room or shared with family's child of the same sex. All homes inspected by local representatives.

Cost $3,100, 6 months; $4,000, 9 months. Covers school enrolment, insurance, supervision, counselling, administration, visas and host family placement.

Medical/accident insurance provided

BELGIUM, CZECH & SLOVAK REPUBLICS, DENMARK, FRANCE, GERMANY, HUNGARY, NETHERLANDS, SWEDEN, SWITZERLAND

Youth For Understanding YFU Office, Unit I D 3, Templeton Business Centre, 62 Templeton Street, Glasgow G40 IDA

0141-556 1116   Fax 0141-551 0949

A non-profitmaking, non-religious, non-political charity, established in 1951 and dedicated to promoting international understanding and world peace through educational exchange programmes

Term stays arranged in Belgium, Czech & Slovak Republics, Denmark, France, Germany, Hungary, Netherlands, Sweden and Switzerland. One academic year, August-July.

Individuals only

Ages 16-18

Four years language study required for French and German speaking countries. Language tuition provided in all other countries.

Students live with a host family and attend the local high school. Training and support for students and host families through extensive volunteer network forms an important part of the programme. Enrichment programme included as part of the programme fee. International seminar for all inter-European students at end of year.

Full board accommodation in family homes. Families are not paid for hosting and students are treated as a family member and not as a guest.

Cost £2,750 covers return travel, residential weekend of training in UK before departure, arrival orientation and language camp, and support services and administration

Group travel where possible. All students are met at airports.

Medical, baggage and liability insurance provided

H

JAPAN, UNITED STATES

Youth For Understanding YFU Office, Unit 1 D 3, Templeton Business Centre, 62 Templeton Street, Glasgow G40 1DA

0141-556 1116   Fax 0141-551 0949

A non-profitmaking, non-religious, non-political charity, established in 1951 and dedicated to promoting international understanding and world peace through educational exchange programmes

Termstays arranged in Japan and the United States. One semester, March-August (Japan) or one academic year, August-July (US).

Individuals only

Ages 16-18

For the programme in Japan, some knowledge of Japanese is preferred, but is not essential if the student is strongly motivated to learn in Japan. Language tuition available.

Students live with a host family and attend full time at the local high school. Training and support for students and host families through extensive volunteers network forms an important part of the programme.

Full board accommodation in family homes. Families are not paid for hosting and students are treated as family members and not as guests.

Cost approx £3,500 (Japan) or £3,750 (US) covers travel from point of departure to host country, internal travel to host family, residential weekend of training in UK before departure, further orientation meetings during the year, support services, administration and language tuition where necessary

Group travel where possible; all students met at airports

Medical, baggage and liability insurance provided

H

WORLDWIDE

Green Theme International Little Rylands Farm, Redmoor, Bodmin, Cornwall PL30 5AR

Bodmin (01208) 873123   Fax Bodmin (01208) 873123

A home exchange company established for travellers who care about the impact of tourism on the environment and culture of their host country and wish to exchange homes with like-minded people

CRA Turismo, Av del Libertador 774 - 5, U, (1001) Buenos Aries, Argentina

Centro Natural, Plaza 18 de Julio, 8, La Villa de Teguise, Lanzarote, Canary Islands

Stéphanie Tamas, 95 Av G Charpentier, La Cougourlude, 34970 Lattes, France

Eurocultura, Via A Rossi 7, 36100 Vicenza, Italy

InterClass, Bori y Fontenstá, 14, 6°, 4°, 08021 Barcelona, Spain

Fair Tours, Postfach 615, 9001 St Gallen, Switzerland

Homestay Zimbabwe, 25 Elizabeth Road, Marlborough, Harare, Zimbabwe

Home exchanges arranged within Britain and in over 35 countries worldwide. As a member of the International Home Exchange Association, Green Theme is also represented in Australia, Canada, Denmark, France, Italy, Spain, Switzerland and the United States.

Annual registration fee £35

Travel insurance available at a discount to members

Membership fee entitles members to have the details of their home listed in one of three annual directories published in November, February and May, and circulated to all members. The introduction to the directory is in five major European languages, giving tips on arranging exchanges. Subscribers also offer hospitality exchange, rentals, bed & breakfast, and student hospitality exchanges.

Computer matching and introductions made to overcome language differences, if requested, for supplementary fee. Airline ticketing service.

BRITAIN, CANADA, UNITED STATES, WORLDWIDE

Home Base Holidays 7 Park Avenue, London N13 5PG

0181-886 8752

A commercial organisation set up in 1986 to run a home exchange service

Home exchanges arranged mainly between Britain and the United States and Canada, but also available worldwide. Member of the International Home Exchange Association (14 member agencies).

Annual membership fee £35

Insurance not provided

Membership fee entitles members to have the details of their home listed in one of three annual directories published in November, February and May and circulated to members. Members also receive a hints booklet on arranging exchanges.

Also publish an annual directory of bed & breakfast reservation agencies and individual host homes in the United States and Canada, £7.

H

AUSTRALIA, CANADA, UNITED STATES, IRELAND, UNITED KINGDOM

Home Exchange PO Box 567, Northampton, Massachusetts 01096, United States

A private organisation set up in 1992 to encourage international travel and contacts by connecting individuals and families for the purpose of home exchange

Home exchanges arranged between the United States and Australia, Canada, Ireland and the UK

Membership fee $50

Four directories published each year, in March, June, October and December. Membership fee entitles members to receive the latest publication and list their information in the following one, which they will also receive. The deadline for information is the last day of the month preceding publication.

H by individual arrangement

WORLDWIDE

HomeLink International Linfield House, Gorse Hill Road, Virginia Water, Surrey GU25 4AS

Ascot (01344) 842642

A worldwide organisation with offices in 32 countries, set up in 1952 to promote the concept of home exchange holidays. The largest home exchange organisation in the world, with about 17,000 members and their families exchanging every year.

Belgium: Jan Klüssendorf, Taxistop, Onderbergen 51, 9000 Gent

Denmark: Dansk Boligbytte, Hesselvang 20, 2900 Hellerup

France: Séjours, Bel Ormeau 409, Avenue Jean Paul-Coste, 13100 Aix-en-Provence

Germany: Holiday Service, Ringstraße 26, 8606 Memmelsdorf I

Ireland: Holiday Exchange International, 95 Bracken Drive, Portmarnock, Co Dublin

Italy: Fiamma Tarchiani, Casa Vacanze, Via San Francesco 170, 35121 Padova

Netherlands: Land Org Vacantie-Woningruil, Kraneveg 86A, 9718 JW, Groningen

Portugal: HomeLink, 100 Rua Vasconceles & Castro 2-d, 4760 V N Famalicao

Spain: Viajes Calatrava, Cea Bermudez 70, 28.003 Madrid

US: Vacation Exchange Club, PO Box 820, Haleiwa, HI 96712

Also has representation in Australia, Canada, Cyprus, Ghana, Israel, Malaysia/Singapore, Namibia, New Zealand, Norway, South Africa, Sweden, Switzerland and the Former Soviet Union

Home exchanges arranged within Britain and in over 50 countries. Members swap homes for an agreed holiday period, usually 2 to 4 weeks.

Annual subscription fee £47 (international directory), £7 (UK only)

30% discount on travel insurance for members

Directory of listings and house photographs covering 55-60 countries and published in five books annually. Subscription entitles members to receive all five, and to list their holiday preferences in the next publication. A separate UK-only directory is published in two books. Details can be updated in later books, and HomeLink runs a computerised late-listing service. Separate, but small, section in directory for youth exchange operations.

H

AFRICA, THE AMERICAS, ASIA, CARIBBEAN, EUROPE, FAR EAST

Interschools Exchange 65 Queens Road, Thame, Oxfordshire OX9 3NF

Thame (01844) 216779

A private, non-profitmaking organisation established in 1993 to provide opportunities for study visits and home exchange for students, teachers, lecturers and their families

Home exchanges can be arranged with members in some 26 different countries worldwide

There are two networks: one covering families and individuals, one covering schools and colleges

Annual subscription fee £25 (within Europe), £28 (outside Europe)

Membership fee entitles members to list their details in brochures published twice a year (end January and end April) and distributed to members with hints on arranging an exchange. In addition to simple house swaps, there are also possibilities for hospitality exchange, student exchange and house-sitting, as well as travelling companions for independent travellers.

AFRICA, ASIA, THE AMERICAS, AUSTRALASIA, EUROPE

Intervac International Home Exchange 3 Orchard Court, North Wraxall, Chippenham, Wiltshire SN14 7AD

Bath (01225) 892208

A private organisation set up in 1953 to enable people to have economical holidays, giving them a real insight into other ways of life

Intervac Australia, Gerd Wilmer, PO Box 7, Manly, NSW 2095, Australia

Intervac Canada, Suzanne Cassin, 606 Alexander Crescent NW, Calgary T2M 4T3, Canada

Intervac France, (Algeria, Morocco and Tunisia), Lucien Mazik, Contacts, 55 rue Nationale, 37000 Tours, France

Intervac Germany, Helge and Dieter Günzler, Verdiweg 2, 7022 Leinfelden-Echterdingen, Germany

Intervac Italy, Gaby Zanobetti, Via Oreglia 18, 40047 Riola (BO), Italy

Intervac Japan, Alain Kregine, 12-27-401 Yochomachi, Shinjuku-Ku, Tokyo 162, Japan

Intervac Spain, Maria Angeles Sas, Consell de Cent, 226, 1°, 3ª, Barcelona, Spain

Intervac US/International Home Exchange Service, Lori Horne and Paula Jaffe, 30 Corte San Fernando, Tiburon, California 94920, United States

Home exchanges in over 40 countries worldwide. Also have representation in Austria, Belgium, Brazil, Denmark, Finland, Greece, Hungary, Iceland, Ireland, Israel, Luxembourg, the Netherlands, Norway, Poland, Portugal, Sweden and Switzerland/Liechtenstein.

Annual membership fee £55

Insurance can be provided at a discount to members

Membership fee entitles members to list their details and requirements in one of three annual directories, and to receive all the books. Details can be updated in later books and the use of a late computer service is also provided. Youth exchange section in directories aimed at young people wanting to plan and organise an exchange project.

H

AFRICA, THE AMERICAS, AUSTRALIA, EUROPE

Teachers House Swaps Star House, Sandford, Crediton, Devon EX17 4LR

Crediton (01363) 774627

A small business set up in 1990 by teachers to provide opportunities for education professionals to exchange homes and visits with other teachers throughout the world, for little more than the cost of travel and insurance

Échanges Enseignants, 6 avenue des Lilas, 64000 Pau, France
© (33) 59 02 30 30   Fax (33) 59 02 93 94

Home exchanges arranged within Britain and with France, the United States, Italy, Germany, Spain, Canada, Sweden, Czech Republic, and possibly Africa, Andorra, Australia, Belgium, Brazil, Costa Rica, Finland, Greece, the Netherlands, Hungary, Latvia, Poland, Portugal, Russia, Switzerland and Turkey

Families wishing to register should have at least one member who is a teacher or education professional

Membership fee £25 (exchanges within the UK) or £40 (worldwide) per year

Membership fee entitles members to print their details in, and receive registers published mid February, late April and possibly June. Deadlines for registration are 1 February and 15 April. New members receive current register and their details are included in next register.

H details of special needs or facilities can be included in registers

AFRICA, ASIA, AMERICAS, AUSTRALASIA, EUROPE

Worldwide Home Exchange Club 50 Hans Crescent, London SW1X 0NA

0171-589 6055

A private organisation set up in 1984 to facilitate home exchanges by listing homes in an annual directory which is circulated to members

Worldwide Home Exchange Club, 806 Brantford Avenue, Silver Spring, MD 20904, United States

Home exchanges available worldwide. Subscribers may opt to rent their home or second home, rather than exchange. Also possibility of a reciprocal hospitality exchange, where members stay in each others' homes as guests.

Annual subscription fee £25. Subscription fee covers home listing and receipt of directory and supplement.

Insurance not provided

A year out, between school and university or work, is a rare chance to stand back, assess where life has brought you so far, and seize the freedom offered to take on a completely different challenge. All the vital advice and information you need to arrange a successful and enjoyable year out is in the Central Bureau guide **A YEAR BETWEEN**.

A YEAR BETWEEN lists over 100 organisations and employers offering year between placements in Britain and 80 other countries. Whatever the opportunity, in whatever country, **the guide** gives very full details. Any age restrictions are noted, the period of work on offer, salary and terms, including whether accommodation, insurance or travel are included is listed, and application deadlines are given together with details of where the work is overseas, and any address in the home country to which application can be made. But we don't stop there.

A YEAR BETWEEN carries information on a wide range of other useful details: a personal checklist covering the pros, cons and options of taking a year out, offering a programmed series of questions to enable participants to

From industrial placements in research in the UK to working on a cattle ranch in Australia; from trekking through Bali, Lombok and Java to tracking Arctic foxes in Norway; from teaching in Spain to working with kids on community projects in Scotland, **A YEAR BETWEEN** has hundreds of opportunities and a wealth of information for a great gap year.

evaluate their potential; authoritative advice on planning & preparation, useful books and other resources; accounts from students and placing organisations alike, providing first hand reports vital to those considering taking a year out; and for potential volunteers, some challenging words on commitment.

A YEAR BETWEEN has opportunities detailed under seven headings: Training/work experience; Discovery/leadership; Conservation/land use; Teaching/ instructing; Community & social service; Youth work/childcare; and Christian service. **The guide** also provides advice on further study options, on travel, insurance and health requirements. In fact, just about everything you'll need to know in order not only to get a successful placement but to make the whole experience worthwhile, fulfilling and as trouble-free as possible.

A YEAR BETWEEN has opportunities for those aged 17+; from 4 weeks up to a whole year; from accountancy placements to zoology expeditions; from Australia to Zimbabwe. For further information on the Bureau's publications and programmes contact the Information Desk on ✆ 0171-725 9448.

A YEAR BETWEEN is published biannually.   Second edition   ISBN 0 900087 98 6   £8.99

PRACTICAL
INFORMATION

BEFORE YOU GO

Although much of the information here is written to assist parent/teachers of a young British person going on a homestay, term stay or exchange, it is equally valid to young people of other nationalities and to older participants.

Before you apply The time it takes to set up a homestay or exchange may vary considerably, but generally speaking it takes longer to arrange an exchange since the matching procedure is of greater importance and an ideal match may take some time. Whatever type of stay you choose, you should allow a period of 2-3 months so that the agency or organisation can find a suitable host family and make all the necessary arrangements. Some organisations insist on a longer period of time; the more notice you are able to give, particularly for exchanges, the better are the chances of having a completely successful stay.

There are more people wishing to learn English than there are British people wanting to learn foreign languages. The majority of British applications will be for stays in France, followed by Germany, Spain then Italy. Therefore applicants from mainland Europe, particularly outside France and Germany, will usually find it takes considerably less time to arrange a homestay than an exchange

Once you have decided on the country to be visited, and have been in touch with a suitable agency or organisation, you should read their literature and application forms very thoroughly. Make sure you know exactly what is covered by the basic fee, for example, what type of insurance cover, if any, is provided, what the travel arrangements are and what provisions are made for illnesses or accidents, or for returning home if serious difficulties should arise. If there are any points on which you are unclear, or if you have any queries, you should contact the agency for clarification. It is obviously wise to have a clear idea of the procedure before an actual application is made.

Preparation Once a match with a suitable host family or exchange partner has been proposed, the applicant should write to them and introduce him/herself. The more contact there is between the families and partners concerned, the easier and more successful will the eventual meeting and subsequent experiences be. Preliminary correspondence is important in learning about the family, the basic social behaviour and the food, for example, in the home to be visited. It can go a long way in helping to minimise the culture shock and homesickness that can often be experienced when there has been little opportunity to learn about the customs and social conventions observed in the other country.

In the case of an exchange of school pupils, the first letter could be in the foreign language, with the teacher helping with any difficulties. Make sure that any letters written in the native language are legible, kept simple and free of spelling or grammar mistakes. Letters should tell the exchange partner about the child, any pets, interests or hobbies, perhaps enclosing a photo of the home or family. All return correspondence should be promptly answered. If it is necessary to telephone the host family to check on arrangements, try to have someone on hand who speaks the language well, or practise what you wish to say.

As a parent, if you or your child have any doubts or worries about the homestay or exchange, or about going abroad generally, try to talk them through. Encourage the student to talk to his/her language teacher or to others who have been on a similar visit. Full preparation for the experience of foreign travel and the different way of life to be encountered is vital if the visit is to be beneficial. Try to teach tolerance and the ability to see another's point of view. Find out as much as possible about the country to be visited; local libraries are a good source of information, and the appropriate tourist office should be able to provide maps and general details on the country and the specific area to be visited. The cultural section of the embassy may also be able to provide information; see the COUNTRY PROFILES section for addresses.

If the student is staying abroad for an extended period or on a term stay, s/he should pay a visit to the doctor and dentist before departure, to reduce any likelihood of falling ill during the stay. Further details of medical preparation are given in this section under **Health**.

What to take Don't pack more than can be comfortably carried, and leave room for any souvenirs or presents that may be brought back. With background information on the host area, investigate the climate and weather patterns so that you are prepared with the right amount and types of clothing. Items such as passports, tickets, money and valuables should not be packed in a suitcase but kept within easy reach in hand luggage. In any case, young people will probably find it easier to pack and carry their belongings in a rucksack rather than a suitcase. It is a nice gesture to take along a small present for the exchange partner or host family, perhaps something typical of your country or locality. Photographs and information about your home area will be of interest to your partner, especially if they are returning your visit. The following checklist, though not exhaustive, may prove helpful:

Passport
Travel tickets
Pocket money
Camera and film(s)
Tourist information
Notebook, address book, pens
Phrase book/pocket dictionary
Sportswear/swimwear
Sun protection items
Comfortable shoes and clothes
Smart clothes for special occasions
Information about your area/country
Prescribed medicines
Form E111
Small gift for your hosts

Pocket money The amount of pocket money required will depend to a great extent on the services covered by the stay. Those opting for homestays with half board, for example, should remember to take enough money to cover the cost of the remaining meal each day. In addition, funds may be required to pay for entrance fees at museums and art galleries, for example, although occasionally such things will be paid for by the host family. In some cases the host family will have been given an allowance to cover extra expenditure such as outings, but this may not always be the case and it is wise to check with the agency to avoid any misunderstandings.

Remember that the cost of living in the country to be visited may be higher than at home, and the organisation should be able to advise on how much money to take to cover expenses. It is also advisable for any visitor to a foreign country to have sufficient funds, preferably in travellers' cheques, to cover unforeseen circumstances. A good guide is to ensure enough is taken to pay for one or two nights' hotel accommodation and a long-distance telephone call. Where necessary, if the money runs out, parents can arrange for money to be transferred to a bank abroad. In a dire emergency, your embassy or consulate in the country you are visiting will be able to advise on funds or help with your travel home if there is no other source of finance available.

Currency Foreign currency can be obtained before departure at major travel agents and *bureau de change* branches of banks; other bank branches may need a few days' notice. You can shop around to get the best exchange rate, but remember that commission is charged on the sale of currency. Some local currency is essential, especially if you are due to arrive at the weekend, but travellers' cheques are safer than cash, and you also get a better rate of exchange. Sterling travellers' cheques are issued by the clearing banks and will need to be ordered at least a week in advance. You will need to show your passport and pay charges. Do not countersign the cheques in advance.

Make a note of the numbers and keep it separate from the cheques; in this way, if you lose the cheques they can still be replaced. Some travellers' cheques can be replaced while you are still abroad, others will be honoured by the issuing bank on your return. If you are visiting North or South America, US$ travellers' cheques can be used as cash.

If you have a current account at a British bank, you will probably be able to obtain a supply of Eurocheques and a cheque card. These cheques can be cashed abroad at banks displaying the Eurocheque sign, and are also accepted in many shops. A small charge may be levied in some countries, and charges may be higher in *bureaux de change*. The cheques are drawn against your current account and are guaranteed up to an agreed amount, usually equivalent to 300 Swiss Francs. Don't forget to take some of your own currency with you for use on the outward and return journeys.

Passports A full UK passport costs £15 and is valid for 10 years. A 94-page passport, useful for those intending to travel through many countries, is available at a cost of £30. Application forms are available at main post offices; completed forms can be sent or taken to your regional passport office (see below). Applications take at least four weeks to process, and can take longer during the summer months and over Christmas; a good guide is to apply at least 3 months in advance.

Passport Office, Clive House, 70-78 Petty France, London SW1H 9HD (personal callers only) ✆ 0171-279 3434

Passport Office, 5th Floor, India Buildings, Water Street, Liverpool L2 0QZ ✆ 0151-237 3010

Passport Office, Olympia House, Upper Dock Street, Newport, Gwent NP9 1XA ✆ Newport (01633) 244500/ 244292

Passport Office, Aragon Court, Northminster Road, Peterborough, Cambridgeshire PE1 1QG ✆ Peterborough (01733) 895555

Passport Office, 3 Northgate, 96 Milton Street, Cowcaddens, Glasgow G4 0BT ✆ 0141-332 0271

Passport Office, Hampton House, 47-53 High Street, Belfast BT1 2QS ✆ Belfast (01232) 232371

Within western Europe and certain other specified countries, British citizens can travel on a British Visitor's Passport (BVP). This costs £7.50 (£11.50 if a spouse is included) but is valid only for 12 months. Application forms are available from any main post office, Monday-Saturday, and should be returned there; in most cases the BVP will be issued immediately. Applicants from Northern Ireland, Jersey, Guernsey and the Isle of Man must obtain them from their area passport office. The BVP can be issued to British citizens, British Dependent Territories citizens and British Overseas citizens for holiday purposes of up to 3 months.

The *Essential Information* booklet contains notes on illness or injury while abroad, insurance, vaccinations, NHS medical cards, consular assistance overseas, British Customs and other useful advice, and is available from all passport offices.

Nationals of other countries will need to consult their own passport-issuing authorities as to the issuing and validity of passports, and should read carefully the details given in the COUNTRY PROFILES section so that they are aware of the entry regulations for the country they plan to visit, and obtain visas where necessary.

If a passport is lost or stolen while abroad, the local police should be notified immediately; if necessary the nearest British Embassy or Consulate will issue a substitute. It is wise to keep a separate note of your passport number.

Visas For entry into some countries, especially in Eastern Europe, a visa or visitor's pass is required, and in many countries a residence permit will be required. See the COUNTRY PROFILES section for further details. Organisations arranging stays in such countries will also be able to advise, and details of application procedures are available from the consular section of the relevant embassy. Regulations are subject to change without warning, and you are advised to obtain precise information before setting out.

Identity cards The International Student Identity Card (ISIC) scheme is operated by the International Student Travel Confederation, a group of major official student bodies worldwide. The card gives internationally accepted proof of student status and consequently ensures that card holders may enjoy many special facilities including fare reductions, cheap accommodation, reduced rates or free entry to museums, art galleries and historical sites. Obtainable from official student travel offices, students' unions and by mail order, the card is available to all full-time students, along with a copy of the *ISIC Handbook*. The card costs £5 and is valid for up to 15 months (1 September-31 December of the following year). For further details call in at your local student travel office or contact ISTC, St Kongensgade 40H, 1264 Copenhagen K, Denmark ℂ (45) 33 11 21 55.

The Federation of International Youth Travel Organisations (FIYTO) aims to promote educational, cultural and social travel amongst young people. The FIYTO International Youth Card is a recognised card offering concessions to young travellers including transport, accommodation, restaurants, excursions, cultural events and reduced rates or free entry to many museums, art galleries, theatres and cinemas. Available to all those between the ages of 12 and 26, together with a booklet giving details of concessions. Available in the UK from Campus Travel offices (London office is at 52 Grosvenor Gardens, London SW1W 0AG ℂ 0171-730 3402).

European Youth Cards are concessionary cards issued by a number of European youth agencies, entitling holders to a range of discounts and special offers on travel, cultural events and goods in high street shops in 18 European countries. Cards are renewable annually, and holders receive a directory of discounters and a regular magazine informing them of new discounts and activities available to card holders. The cards are available from the following organisations:

England and Wales: Under 26 Card available from Under 26, 52 Grosvenor Gardens, London SW1W 0AG ℂ 0171-823 5363. Cost £6.

Scotland: Young Scot Card available from some tourist boards, theatres and youth information centres, and from the Scottish Community Education Council, Rosebery House, 9 Haymarket Terrace, Edinburgh EH12 5EZ ℂ 0131-313 2488. Cost £6.

Northern Ireland: European Youth Card available from USIT, Fountain Centre, Belfast BT1 6ET ℂ Belfast (01232) 324073, and other USIT offices. Cost £6.

Ireland: European Youth Card available from USIT, Aston Quay, O'Connell Bridge, Dublin 2 ℂ Dublin (1) 778117, and other USIT offices. Cost IR£6.

Health Changes in food and climate may cause minor illnesses, and, especially when visiting the hotter countries of southern Europe, Africa, Latin America and the Far East it is wise to take extra care in your hygiene, eating and drinking habits. Local bacteria, to which native inhabitants are immune, may cause the visitor stomach upsets, so it is worth avoiding tap water and doing without ice in your drinks. In a hot climate never underestimate the strength of the sun, or overestimate your own strength. Drink plenty of fluid, make sure there is enough salt in your diet, wear loose-fitting cotton clothes, even a hat, take things easy and guard against heat exhaustion, heat stroke and sunburn. This advice may sound overcautious, but it would be a shame to let the climate spoil your homestay or exchange.

In the UK the Department of Health issues leaflet *T4 Health Advice for Travellers*, available from post offices, travel agents, libraries and doctors' surgeries. This include details of compulsory and recommended vaccinations, other measures that can be taken to protect one's health, information on rabies, AIDS, malaria and other diseases. There is also advice on types of food and on water supplies which may be a source of infection.

A certificate of vaccination against certain diseases is an entry requirement for some countries. See the COUNTRY PROFILES section for further details, or consult the relevant embassy as such requirements are continually subject to review.

A general recommendation is to make sure that your protection against typhoid, polio and tetanus is up-to-date if you are travelling outside Europe, North America or Australasia. Up-to-the-minute printouts indicating the immunisations and malaria tablets appropriate for any specific journey are available from the Medical Advisory Service to Travellers Abroad (MASTA). By calling them on 0891 224100 you can leave a recorded message listing countries you will be visiting, the month of arrival in each, and the living conditions (rural, towns, cities, business, tourist). The required information will be sent by return; calls are charged at 39p/49p per minute (cheap rate/all other times). MASTA printouts are also available without charge for those attending British Airways travel clinics throughout Britain; for details of the one nearest to you call 0171-831 5333. Remember that protection against some diseases takes the form of a course of injections over several weeks, so allow plenty of time.

If you are taking prescribed drugs it is advisable to carry a doctor's letter giving details of the medical condition and the medication, avoiding the possibility of confusion. It will also be useful to find out the generic rather than the brand name of the medicine, so that if need arises further supplies can be obtained abroad.

Even if you are visiting a country where the climate is similar to your own, you may still find the first few days rather a strain. This is understandable, especially if you are away from home for the first time. Adapting to a new environment and to communicating in a foreign language can put you under quite a lot of pressure, with the result that you may feel easily tired and drained. If you take things easy and get plenty of rest you should soon get back to normal.

Reciprocal health arrangements
You are only covered by the NHS whilst in the UK, and may therefore have to pay the full costs of any treatment abroad. However, there are health care arrangements between all European Union (EU) countries (Belgium, Britain, Denmark, France, Germany, Greece, Ireland, Italy, Luxembourg, the Netherlands, Portugal and Spain). British citizens resident in the UK will receive free or reduced cost emergency treatment in other EU countries on production of form E111 which includes leaflet T4 Health Advice for Travellers (see above). This leaflet explains who is covered by the arrangements, what treatment is free or at reduced cost, and gives the procedures which must be followed to get treatment in countries where form E111 is not needed (usually Denmark, Ireland and Portugal). Form E111 is issued with information on how to get emergency medical treatment in other EU countries. Form E111 must be taken abroad and, if emergency treatment is needed, the correct procedures must be followed.

There are also reciprocal health care arrangements between Britain and Australia, Austria, Barbados, Bulgaria, Channel Islands, the Czech and Slovak Republics, Finland, Gibraltar, Hong Kong, Hungary, Iceland, Isle of Man,

Malta, New Zealand, Norway, Poland, Romania, Sweden, former republics of the USSR, the former Yugoslavia and the British Dependent Territories of Anguilla, British Virgin Islands, Falkland Islands, Montserrat, St Helena, and Turks and Caicos Islands. However, private health insurance may still be needed in these countries; leaflet *T4* gives full details

.

Despite reciprocal health arrangements it is still essential to take out full medical insurance whenever travelling overseas. The health treatment available in other countries may not be as comprehensive as in the UK, and none of the arrangements listed above cover the cost of repatriation in the event of illness.

Insurance You must find out from the organisation arranging your stay whether they provide insurance cover against risk of accident, illness and possible disability. Many organisations either include insurance cover in the price of their homestay/exchange package or can arrange it at additional cost. It is important to ascertain exactly what is included in the cover offered, as frequently it is limited to third party risk or public liability. Third party risk only provides cover for persons other than the individual concerned, while public liability concerns injury to people or damage to property arising from carelessness on the part of the company concerned. The homestay or exchange organisation should be able to advise, but it is up to you to decide exactly what extent of insurance cover you require. A typical holiday insurance package will cover cancellation and delay, medical and emergency travel expenses, personal accident, loss of luggage and money, and personal liability.

The International Student Insurance Service (ISIS) policy is a leading policy for young travellers and provides, at competitive rates, a wide range of benefits covering death, disablement, medical and other personal expenses, loss of luggage, personal liability and cancellation, loss of deposits or curtailment. An advantage of this policy is that medical expenses can be settled on the spot in many countries by student organisations cooperating with ISIS. A 24-hour assistance service is provided to handle all medical emergencies. Details in the UK from 150 local Endsleigh Insurance centres (see *Yellow Pages* for details).

Travel Some organisations are happy to make or advise on all necessary travel/escort arrangements, although this service is not always included in the price. Other organisations expect individuals to make their own way to a particular point of departure where they will then join a group. The cost of travel to the point of departure would then be the responsibility of the individual. On arrival in the host country, participants are either met by the host families or local representatives, or make their own way to the town where they will be staying, in some cases at their own cost.

For those making their own travel arrangements, there are a number of specialist operators and low-cost tickets available for young people; details are given in the COUNTRY PROFILES section. It is advisable to book only with those travel agents who are members of the Association of British Travel Agents (ABTA) or the International Association of Travel Agents (IATA), and when reserving flights, to book only with agents who hold an Air Travel Organisers Licence (ATOL).

Visitors to Britain are normally met at the point of arrival by a representative or by the host family. Where this is not the case, you should make your own way from the port or airport to an arranged meeting place. Both London Heathrow and Gatwick airports are well served by public transport. On arrival, ask at the information desk for advice. Major sea ports in Britain are served by good rail and road links with the rest of the country.

Customs If you are going to be spending time abroad you should be aware of the Customs regulations governing the host country. A good country guidebook or a brochure from the relevant tourist office will be able to advise on the regulations in force. Details of UK Customs regulations are given in the various *Customs Public Notices* available from Customs & Excise local offices or from Customs at ports and airports in the UK. Persons under 17 are not entitled to tobacco or drinks allowances. There are prohibitions and restrictions on the importation of certain goods ranging from drugs and weapons to foodstuffs and plants. On arrival in the UK, persons with goods in excess of their duty and tax-free allowances or who are in doubt, should declare the goods in the red clearance channel. Further information may be obtained from local Customs enquiry offices or from HM Customs & Excise Advice Centre, Dorset House, Stamford Street, London SEI 9NG ✆ 0171-202 4227.

Problems Should you lose your ticket at the last minute, you should contact the airline/shipping company/tour operator immediately to see if a replacement can be issued. If luggage is lost during a flight and does not turn up on arrival at the foreign destination, the duty officer of the airline concerned should be informed immediately. If the luggage cannot be traced, a claim form must be completed. Most airlines will immediately provide a small payment to cover necessities, but they are under no obligation to do so, and the amount varies considerably from airline to airline. This payment does not usually have to be repaid if the luggage is traced. If after 3-4 weeks the luggage still has not been found, compensation will be paid by the airline according to the declaration made on the claim form. In any event, and to cover loss on other means of transport, it is advisable to take out a personal insurance policy which covers luggage loss. Any losses should of course be reported to the insurance company concerned.

WHILE YOU'RE THERE

Code of conduct You should try to be as friendly and cheerful as possible. If you start off with a positive attitude, you will find it much easier to get on with your host family. If you are meeting your exchange partner for the first time, bear in mind that the agency has made every effort to match you according to interests and personality, so you should have a lot in common. But don't expect to be best friends from the moment you first meet; it takes time and patience to get to know someone, so make allowances for this.

It is important to remember that you are a guest in someone's home, and that the host family is responsible for your welfare during the stay. Their ideas on how young people should behave may well differ from those of your parents, but in the interests of harmony you should try to accept them. Consider yourself as an ambassador; your attitudes and behaviour will inevitably influence the impression your host family have of your country. The agency may also have rules they wish you to follow, and these should be made clear to you beforehand. Try also to bear the following guidelines in mind:

✗ Don't go out alone or with friends, even during the day, without asking permission and explaining where you are going. If you have to be back by a certain time, then don't be late.

✓ Offer to help with household chores, such as clearing the table or washing up.

✓ Keep your bedroom tidy, make your own bed and always clear up after yourself.

✗ Don't make telephone calls without asking permission, and do offer to pay for them.

✗ Don't smoke or drink alcohol unless you have permission to do so. These habits may well be forbidden by the agency in any case.

✓ Spend time with your host family. Don't mope in your bedroom or they will worry that you are unhappy or ill.

✓ Be communicative, even if you are shy. Show enthusiasm and express your opinions. If you don't make the effort you are unlikely to improve your knowledge of the language, and you may well have a miserable time.

✓ Above all, be considerate, helpful and polite.

Food Often you will be asked by the agency to specify any food which is part of your dietary requirements or which you do not like, but remember that learning about food and customs is an important part of a homestay, so you should try to be open to new tastes and experiences.

Laundry Some host families will be quite willing to do your washing for you, but they are by no means obliged to do so. Check beforehand with the agency, and ask permission from the host family if you want to do some washing for yourself.

Language Once you've arrived you may be surprised to find your foreign language ability wasn't quite as good as you thought. It is always much easier to read a foreign language, or do the exercises in a textbook, than it is to carry on a conversation with someone who is using words you do not know or talking too quickly for you. You may also get tired because you have to listen extra carefully in order to understand. The answer is to be patient and persevere. By the end of the stay you will be using words you never knew before! The following tips may help:

- Don't be afraid to ask questions. Get people to speak more slowly or repeat what they have said.

- Carry a pocket dictionary with you.

- Make a note of new words and expressions.

- Watch children's TV; get young children to help you practise their language. They're learning too, and it could be fun to learn with them.

- Try to avoid speaking your own language. The more practice you have in the foreign language, the better.

- Above all, relax. Everyone makes mistakes!

Adjusting to your new environment
It is only natural to feel homesick for the first day or so, especially if this is your first time away from home. Moping around will not help, and if you phone your parents you may end up missing them even more, not to mention worrying them. The only cure is to put a brave face on it and throw yourself into any activities that your host family are organising.

If your stay is for an extended period, such as a term stay, you may experience difficulties in adjusting to the cultural experience, or culture shock. At the beginning of your stay, although you may miss your home environment, you are likely to find everything very new and exciting, and you'll spend perhaps the first month or so on a high. As the excitement fades, you may experience anxiety, tiredness, irritability, depression and homesickness. The stresses of working hard to communicate in another language, trying to decipher a difficult accent, making an effort to be polite and adapt to what may seem an alien culture, will all combine to get you down. You will probably feel that your mood has been brought on by other people: you've been making every effort to be flexible and courteous, it's just all these foreigners who are making life difficult for you. This low point, which can last up to three weeks or more, is all the worse considering the excitement you felt when you first arrived.

The best way of dealing with culture shock is firstly to expect it to happen - if it doesn't, then count yourself lucky! Try to stand back from your feelings and realise what is happening to you and why. It is tiring to communicate with people who don't speak the same language as you, and coming to terms with another culture can be really difficult, as it challenges beliefs, customs and codes of conduct that you've been absorbing and accepting since birth. So it's only natural for you to feel stressed, but do your best not to give in to negative feelings. View it rather as a positive experience - at least it means that you are starting to become aware of cultural differences. Relax, learn to accept the ways of life of your host country, without forgetting your own. As you become more attuned to your new environment, so the culture shock will pass.

Problems A well-organised homestay or exchange should pose few problems. The organisations and agencies in this guide will make every effort to ensure that any difficulties which do arise are dealt with quickly and efficiently. Many have local representatives and it is important you have their address and telephone number. It is worth clarifying beforehand what the procedure would be should you find that you wished to terminate the stay earlier than planned. If, for example, you have made a genuine effort to overcome difficulties, but still do not get on with your host family, it may be possible to arrange alternative accommodation.

Where an exchange is involved, should either party feel they do not want to complete the exchange, some kind of agreement will have to be reached concerning payment for hospitality already provided. In some cases it may be possible to find another exchange partner; such negotiations are best handled by the organisation arranging the stay.

In case of real emergencies, it is a good idea to have with you addresses and telephone numbers of your country's embassy or consulate in the host country. Details of these can be found in the COUNTRY PROFILES section. British Consuls maintain a list of English-speaking doctors and will help in cases of serious difficulties. As a last resort, a consul can arrange for a direct return to the UK by the cheapest possible passage, providing the individual surrenders his/her passport and gives a written undertaking to pay the travel expenses involved. The telegraphic address of all British embassies is *Prodrome*, and of all British consulates *Britain*, followed in each case by the name of the appropriate town.

If you are dissatisfied with the handling of the stay you should put your complaint in writing to the organisation concerned. Although the Central Bureau for Educational Visits and Exchanges has taken up references for the organisations listed in this guide, it cannot accept responsibility for their subsequent conduct. The Central Bureau would appreciate, however, being informed of any problems so that complaints can be recorded and investigated. Up-to-date reports enable us to improve the standard and accuracy of the information given here, and when you have been on a stay, the completion and return of the REPORT FORM (at the back of this guide) would be appreciated.

Many of the organisations operating in Britain are members of a regional tourist board. This means that they must ask host families to comply with the British Tourist Authority code of conduct with reference to family accommodation. Where problems are encountered it is advisable to inform the relevant tourist board as soon as possible.

GUIDELINES

Host families A host family welcomes a visitor not just into their home, but into their life. The guest learns about the family's attitudes and values by participating in their daily routine, while in turn the family learns about the visitor's way of life. If you are considering hosting foreign visitors yourself, and are willing to provide a little more than just accommodation, you should contact an organisation which arranges stays in your area to see if they would be willing to consider you as a host.

The majority of the agencies in this guide specialise in stays for young people, so families with children are particularly welcome. However, if you do not have children, or if you wish to receive adult guests, you will still be welcomed by many suitable agencies. A representative will visit you in your home and will ask for details of your family and interests, so that they can match you with a suitable guest. You may find it helpful to talk to other families who have already hosted a visitor.

Many agencies will have guidelines for hosting which they will expect you to follow. For example you will probably be requested not to have another guest of the same nationality in the house; this is understandable - guests are there to learn your language, not to talk in their own. There may also be rules regarding accommodation; in some cases single bedrooms are stipulated. Most guests will appreciate time in their own room occasionally, either to write letters, read, or just rest - it is quite a strain to speak a foreign language all day. Abide by the rules laid down by the agency; your guests will be expecting certain standards and may complain to the agency if they find these standards are not being met.

Hosting should not be undertaken lightly. It can be very demanding; many agencies expect their families to involve their guests in activities and take them on outings. There should be a genuine desire on your part to welcome a visitor as part of your family. It is not to be undertaken with only an idea of profit in mind; in fact you may very well find yourself spending more money than usual while your visitor is with you. However, it is undoubtedly a rewarding experience, and one which many families are happy to repeat.

Preparation If you or your child are to make the first contact with your guest, send them a cheerful introductory letter in good time. Get the whole family involved in planning outings and activities. Make sure your guest has a bright, tidy, welcoming room to stay in, with adequate space for clothes. It is important to give your guest a friendly welcome; this is bound to reassure any anxious visitor who may be abroad for the first time. Bear in mind that they may be tired and hungry after their journey and a barrage of questions in a foreign language is not likely to help them relax. A hot drink and bed may be just what they need. For the first day or so they may feel tired, disorientated and possibly homesick. This is understandable; don't feel that it is due to a failure on your part to make them feel at home. It will soon pass if you keep them occupied and show understanding and affection.

Explain to your guest the layout and rules of your household. Don't change your family routine to suit your guest; it is their responsibility to adapt to your way of life, so everyone in the family should just act naturally.

Language Make allowances for your guest's unfamiliarity with your language. Speak slowly, avoiding too many slang or colloquial expressions, as these will not help them improve their vocabulary. They may sound blunt or rude at times, but this will only be because they don't understand the subtleties of your language yet. Misunderstandings will almost inevitably occur, but treat these with good humour; if your guest can laugh with you at mistakes then nobody need get embarrassed. Only correct major mistakes; if every little error is corrected your guest will be afraid to talk, whereas encouragement and praise will work wonders. Remember that no matter how intelligent a person is, they may feel stupid, shy and cut off when struggling to understand a different language and trying to express their thoughts clearly. Involve your guest in every conversation, don't let them feel left out.

Food Make sure your guest knows the family mealtimes and keeps to them. Eating with the host family is the ideal opportunity for conversation. Do not worry about preparing special foods, as your guest should want to try national and local specialities, but it is advisable to check for likes and dislikes. You could always offer your guest the chance to cook a meal typical of their own country, perhaps as a farewell dinner - this could be a good way for you to find out about their culture.

Activities You may be surprised what simple things please your guest; things you take for granted may be things your guest has never experienced before. Try and think what activities typical of your country may interest them, like riding on top of a London double-decker bus, or even eating fish and chips. Involve your guest in the discussion and take their interests into account. They may not be interested in visiting the local museum, but the idea of a picnic on top of a nearby hill or a trip to the seaside may be very appealing. Don't be afraid to ask their opinion.

Treat young guests in general as you would your own children. If they are old enough, allow them to go out on their own, as long as this is within the agency's guidelines, but make sure you know where they are going and when they'll be back. Don't take offence if they're keen to go out alone; it's a new experience for them, so try suggesting places they can visit. Make sure they know about public transport, and that they've got your phone number in case they get lost. It probably isn't a good idea, though, to give them your house key and let them come and go as they please.

Home exchanges Home exchange is becoming an increasingly popular holiday concept. The advantages are clear: rent-free accommodation, far less restricting than staying in a hotel, and without the worry of leaving your own home empty while you are away. If you exchange with a home abroad you get the real cultural experience of living in a typical home as part of the local community.

Many home exchange agencies operate as clubs. In exchange for an annual membership fee you advertise your home in one or more directories from which you select homes you would like to exchange with. Initial contact with potential home exchange partners is then usually made by phone or in writing. Some agencies do the matching for you, through a computer network or by means of local coordinators based in the relevant country. In this case an administration fee is usually charged, plus a further fee once a suitable exchange home has been found.

Agreeing on an exchange Once an exchange has been decided upon a clear agreement should be made in writing, in order to avoid any possible misunderstandings. Confirm arrival and departure dates and agree now on arrangements to be made if, in the case of an emergency, either side has to return home early or even cancel. The agency may be able to help find a replacement but this cannot be guaranteed. Some holiday insurance policies may cover you for any costs that arise in this case.

Discuss which bills should be paid by whom; the simplest arrangement is probably for householders themselves to pay gas/electricity bills and for guests to keep a record of telephone calls and pay at the end of their stay. Agree on duties such as looking after pets, mowing the lawn or watering plants. If you intend to swap cars, agree on what should happen and who should pay in the case of repairs, breakdowns or accidents. If you have any valuables or items that you do not wish to be used, then inform your partner. It is a good idea to lock such items out of harm's way, but remember home exchangers will always treat other people's property with respect; after all, they're in the same position as you are. Finally, make sure you agree where the keys will be left, usually with a friend or neighbour.

Insurance Always inform your insurance company that you are exchanging your home, as it may affect the cover. The same applies if you are swapping your car; there may be an extra premium to cover a foreign driver, and the insurance company may wish to have details of their driving history. Let your exchange partner have full details of all insurance policies, and find out about theirs to ensure that you too are adequately covered when using their home and car.

Welcoming your guests Make sure your exchange partner knows how to get to your house, and arrange for a friend or neighbour to meet them when they arrive. Give them your friend's phone number in case they are late or get lost. Clean your home thoroughly, make the beds and leave plenty of space in wardrobes and drawers. Make sure there are supplies of tea, coffee, milk, sugar, toilet paper, light bulbs and other basics to last at least for the first day or two, and if they are arriving late at night leave food for them to cook a meal. A nice gesture could be to leave a bunch of flowers by way of welcome. Look out instruction manuals for household appliances, and your car manual if this is part of the exchange. You should also compile a list of basic information and leave it in a prominent place. This should include details such as:

✓ Emergency telephone numbers, including your doctor, dentist, vet, electrician, plumber, local garage and insurance broker.

✓ Where to turn off gas, electricity and water, and where to find a toolbox.

✓ When the refuse collectors will call.

✓ Which doors and windows should be

locked at night or when they go away.

✓ Local information such as where to shop, early closing day, pubs, restaurants, cinemas, tourist attractions and sports facilities. Maps and street plans are also useful, as is information on local public transport.

After the exchange Leave your partner's home exactly as you found it; they will do the same for you. Try to put everything back in its proper place, and make sure you leave basic food and supplies - they'll be very irritated to return home and find you've used the last tea-bag!

Other homestays Apart from the homestays already given in this guide, a number of schemes exist where one can live and work abroad, very often on a farm, in a family setting. These programmes should not be classed as holidays, as you are expected to work; however they still offer valuable opportunities for finding out about family life in another country.

The International Farm Experience Programme provides assistance to young farmers and nurserymen by finding places in farms/nurseries abroad, enabling them to broaden their agricultural knowledge. Placements are offered in Australia, Austria, Belgium, Bulgaria, Canada, China, the Czech Republic, Denmark, Finland, France, Germany, Greece, Hungary, Israel, Italy, Luxembourg, the Netherlands, New Zealand, Norway, Poland, Portugal, Spain, Sweden, Switzerland and the United States. Participants live and work with a farming family, and the work is matched as far as possible with the participant's requirements. Applicants should be aged 18-28, have a valid driving licence, at least 2 years'

practical experience, 1 year of which may be at agricultural college, and intend to make a career in agriculture/ horticulture.

The International Agricultural Exchange Association provides opportunities for young people involved in agriculture, horticulture or home management to acquire practical work experience and improve their understanding of life in other countries. Participants are given an opportunity to study practical methods in other parts of the world on approved training farms and work as trainees, gaining further experience in their chosen field. Opportunities exist in Australia, Canada, Japan, New Zealand and the United States. Applicants should be aged 18-30, single, have good practical experience plus a valid driving licence.

Further details of the above schemes available from the respective organisation at the National Agricultural Centre, Stoneleigh Park, Kenilworth, Warwickshire CV8 2LG.

Working as an au pair is another way to spend some time abroad, study a foreign language and achieve an awareness of life in another country. An au pair is treated as a member of the family and in return for board, lodging and pocket money is expected to help with light household duties, including the care of any children, for a maximum of 30 hours per week. There should be sufficient spare time to make friends, go sightseeing and take a part-time language course. Further details of agencies offering placements in Britain and abroad together with details of the legislation governing au pairs can be found in *Working Holidays*, the Central Bureau's annual international guide to seasonal job opportunities.

Other exchanges The term *exchange* can have a very broad meaning, and does not simply refer to the reciprocal family stays outlined in this guide. There are many types of exchange scheme in operation, covering work experience and observation, study visits and cultural exchanges. Many of them are the result of formal agreements between governments with quotas for participants in any given year.

Further details of all the exchange schemes outlined below, together with information on the whole range of programmes and services offered by the Central Bureau, are available from the Central Bureau for Educational Visits and Exchanges, Seymour Mews House, Seymour Mews, London W1H 9PE ✆ 0171-486 5101.

The Central Bureau operates teacher exchange schemes with Austria, Belgium, Denmark, France, Germany, Italy, Spain, Switzerland, the United States and the former Soviet Union. The majority of the exchanges (except for those with the United States) are for teachers of modern languages, although teachers of other subjects are eligible to apply. The length of appointment varies from 3 weeks to a full academic year. Teachers exchange posts with an overseas colleague and return to their own posts following the exchange. Depending on circumstances, teachers may also wish to swap accommodation for the duration of the exchange. Unilateral exchange posts are also available for English teachers in Bulgaria and for teachers of physics in Romania.

The Central Bureau is the UK office of the International Association for the Exchange of Students for Technical Experience (IAESTE), which runs an exchange scheme providing undergraduate students with course-related technical or commercial experience in another country. IAESTE covers a wide range of subject fields and operates in North and South America, Europe, the Middle East, Asia and Australia. Placements last from 8-12 weeks to a year. Students pay their own travel expenses; a salary is paid by the firm. Students usually apply through their own university or college, which should be affiliated to the national IAESTE office.

A class link is a twinning between two classes in different countries, where correspondence and exchange projects can be used to enrich the curriculum, particularly in the areas of European/ world studies, history, geography and modern languages. Under the guidance of their teacher a class or group might exchange letters, photographs, audio/ video cassettes, joint project work and all types of educational material with a class abroad. Penfriend links between individual pupils can also be established, the teachers matching pupils' ages and interests. Links involving modern languages in particular, frequently lead to group or individual exchange visits. British links with English-speaking countries, for example the United States, are useful in developing pupils' practical ability to express themselves as well as an invaluable opportunity to explore a new culture.

A school link is a twinning between two schools in different countries. The teachers responsible organise various activities enabling the pupils to learn about each other's country and way of life through personal contact. This very often starts with pupils exchanging letters, and frequently leads to individual or group exchange visits. Generally speaking, the aim of these school exchanges is to increase the knowledge and understanding of the lifestyle and culture of other countries. The benefits both to the individual and to the school as a whole are immeasurable, widening the students' horizons and encouraging them to explore and share special interests such as music and sports.

The Central Bureau can, with the cooperation of ministries of education abroad, find suitable partner schools for those in the UK wishing to set up a school or class link. Links with countries whose language is taught in British schools are especially popular but the Central Bureau also receives requests for links from other EU countries, Scandinavia, eastern Europe and the United States.

There can be financial, organisational and other advantages if links form part of a broader exchange such as a partnership or twinning between towns, districts or counties. The Joint Twinning Committee of the Local Authority Associations of Great Britain and Northern Ireland, based at the Local Government International Bureau, 35 Great Smith Street, London SW1P 3BJ ℗ 0171-222 1636 maintains a register of civic twinnings and can offer help and advice to local authorities and twinning associations seeking partners abroad. The Central Bureau for Educational Visits and Exchanges can also link local education authorities with counterparts abroad; links may be based on an existing civic twinning or on the initiative of education officers seeking a relevant partner.

The Youth Exchange Centre was established by the British government to promote international youth exchanges through the provision of advice,

information, training and grants. It is the UK National Agency for the European Union programme Youth for Europe, established to promote youth exchanges between the EU member states. It provides grant aid to UK youth groups to assist in their outward travel costs and the costs involved in hosting their partner group. It has established a network of 12 Regional Committees who make decisions on most applications for grant awards and provide a localised information and training service on all aspects of youth exchanges. Support is available for youth exchanges with EU member states, the rest of western Europe, east European countries, the United States and Japan. Further information from the Youth Exchange Centre, British Council, 10 Spring Gardens, London SW1A 2BN ℗ 0171-389 4030.

COUNTRY PROFILES

ARGENTINA

Argentine Embassy 53 Hans Place, London SW1X 0LA © 0171-584 6494 Fax 0171-589 3106

British Embassy Dr Luis Agote 2412/52 (Casilia de Correo 2050), 1425 Buenos Aires, Argentina © (54 1) 803 7070/1

Electricity 220 volts AC

Currency The Peso, divided into 100 centavos. Approx 1.5 Pesos to £1. US dollars and travellers' cheques widely accepted.

Health Travellers advised to take precautions against cholera, typhoid and malaria

Time GMT -3 hours

Travel The following companies can arrange low-cost flights to Argentina, and may also be able to help with internal travel, insurance and tours:

Campus Travel, offices throughout the UK, including a student travel centre at 52 Grosvenor Gardens, London SW1W 0AG © 0171-730 8111 or © 0131-668 3303 for Scottish telephone bookings.

Council Travel, 28A Poland Street, London W1V 3DB © 0171-437 7767 (offices also in Paris, Nice, Lyon, Munich, Düsseldorf, Tokyo, Singapore and throughout the US).

North-South Travel, Moulsham Mill, Parkway, Chelmsford CM2 7PX © Chelmsford (01245) 492882. All profits are given to projects in the developing world.

STA Travel, 86 Old Brompton Road, London SW7 3LQ/117 Euston Road, London NW1 2SX © 0171-937 9962 (offices also in Birmingham, Bristol, Cambridge, Glasgow, Leeds, Manchester and Oxford).

Useful publications Lonely Planet's *Argentina, Uruguay & Paraguay - A Travel Survival Kit* £10.95 and *South America on a Shoestring* £16.95 offer practical information for budget travellers wanting to explore beyond the usual tourist routes.

Michael's Guide to South America £13.95 is detailed and concise, providing invaluable practical advice for all kinds of travellers. Published by Inbal Travel. Available from good bookshops.

Entry regulations Visas are required for most visitors, except citizens from the bordering countries of Brazil, Chile, Paraguay and Uruguay

AUSTRALIA

Australian High Commission Australia House, The Strand, London WC2B 4LA © 0891 600333

Australian Tourist Commission Gemini House, 10-18 Putney Hill, Putney, London SW15 6AA © 0181-780 1424

British High Commission Commonwealth Avenue, Yarralumla, Canberra ACT 2600, Australia © (61 6) 270 6666. Consulates-General in Adelaide, Brisbane, Melbourne, Perth and Sydney.

British Tourist Authority 8th Floor, University Centre, 210 Clarence Street, Sydney, NSW 2000, Australia © (61 2) 267 4555 Fax (61 2) 267 4442

Electricity 240/250 volts AC

Currency The Australian Dollar (A$), divided into 100 cents. Approx A$2.10 to £1.

Health Certificate of inoculation against yellow fever required if travelling from or through infected area

Time GMT +8 to +11 hours

Travel The Australian Coachlines Bus Pass offers unlimited travel on Australia's largest express route, with discounts on accommodation, sightseeing and car rental. Cost A$343 (7 days) or A$600 (14 days). Details from Greyhound International, Sussex House, London Road, East Grinstead RH19 1LD ✆ East Grinstead (01342) 317317 Fax (01342) 328519, or from Long-Haul Leisurail, see below.

Austrailpass entitles the holder to unlimited travel on Rail Australia. 14-90 days from £218. Details from Long-Haul Leisurail, PO Box 113, Bretton, Peterborough PE3 8HY ✆ Peterborough (01733) 335599.

The following companies can arrange low-cost flights to Australia, and may also be able to help with internal travel, insurance and tours:

Campus Travel, offices throughout the UK including a student travel centre at 52 Grosvenor Gardens, London SW1W 0AG ✆ 0171-730 8111 or ✆ 0131-668 3303 for Scottish telephone bookings.

Council Travel, 28A Poland Street, London W1V 3DB ✆ 0171-437 7767 (offices also in Paris, Nice, Lyon, Munich, Düsseldorf, Tokyo, Singapore and throughout the US).

North-South Travel, Moulsham Mill, Parkway, Chelmsford CM2 7PX ✆ Chelmsford (01245) 492882. All profits given to projects in the developing world.

STA Travel, 86 Old Brompton Road, London SW7 3LQ/117 Euston Road, London NW1 2SX ✆ 0171-937 9962 (offices also in Birmingham, Bristol, Cambridge, Glasgow, Leeds, Manchester and Oxford).

Entry regulations All travellers (except Australian and New Zealand passport holders) need a visa, which should be applied for well in advance of departure.

Useful publications The Australian Tourist Commission, see above, publish *Australia - A Traveller's Guide,* a comprehensive booklet including all the facts needed to plan a trip.

Lonely Planet's *Australia - A Travel Survival Kit* £13.95 offers practical, down-to-earth information for budget travellers wanting to explore beyond the usual tourist routes.

The Rough Guide to Australia £12.99 provides comprehensive background information, with details on getting there, getting around and places to explore.

Culture Shock! Australia £6.95 introduces the reader to the people, ceremonies, customs, food and cultures of Australia, with checklists of dos and don'ts.

Travellers Survival Kit Australia & New Zealand £9.95 gives information on travelling as cheaply as possible, local culture, pubs and restaurants, beaches and reefs. Published by Vacation Work, 9 Park End Street, Oxford OX1 1HJ ✆ Oxford (01865) 241978.

Bed & breakfast/Farm accommodation The Australian Tourist Commission, see above, can provide lists of organisations arranging bed & breakfast and farm accommodation; some are listed below.

Ausres, Suite 1, 27-33 Raglan Street, South Melbourne, Victoria 3205, Australia ✆ (61 3) 699 5577 Fax (61 3) 696 0329 offers a central booking service for homestays and farmstays.

Australian Farmhost Holidays Pty, PO Box 65, Culcairn, NSW 2660, Australia ✆ (61 60) 298621 organises farmstays and farm holidays throughout Australia. Prices range from A$23-A$135. UK agent: Gold Medal Travel, Metropolitan Drive, Preston New Road, Blackpool FY3 9LT ✆ Blackpool (01253) 798181 Fax (01253) 791333.

Bed & Breakfast Australia, PO Box 408, Gordon, NSW 2072, Australia ✆ (61 2) 498 5344 Fax (61 2) 498 6438 are agents for bed & breakfast accommodation in most major cities and some country towns; average A$50 per person per night. Also farmstays throughout Australia; A$110 per person per day including all meals.

Farm Holidays, 98 Fletcher Street, Woollahra, NSW 2025, Australia ✆ (61 2) 387 6681 Fax (66 2) 387 8121 can supply details of hosts for homestays and farmstays.

Heritage Tasmania Pty Ltd, PO Box 780 Sandy Bay, Tasmania 7005, Australia ✆ (61 02) 241612 Fax (61 02) 240472 can arrange homestays and farmstays, self-contained and heritage accommodation.

Houseguest, 4/5 Ward Place, Dural, NSW 2158, Australia ✆ (61 2) 651 3177 Fax (61 2) 651 2363 offers bed & breakfast accommodation in all state capitals and tourist destinations. Homes are located in suburban areas, farms, vineyards and cattle stations. UK agent: Australian Destination Centre, Ryedale Building, Piccadilly, York YO1 1PN ✆ York (01904) 611890 Fax (01904) 611896.

Host Farms Association Inc, 332 Banyule Road, View Bank 3084, Victoria, Australia ✆ (61 3) 457 5413 Fax (61 3) 457 6725 is an agency for farm accommodation throughout Victoria. H some farms have wheelchair accessible accommodation.

AUSTRIA

Austrian Embassy 18 Belgrave Mews West, London SW1X 8HU ✆ 0171-235 3731

Austrian National Tourist Office 30 St George Street, London W1R 0AL ✆ 0171-629 0461 Fax 0171-499 6038

British Embassy Jaurèsgasse 12, 1030 Vienna ✆ (43 1) 7131574/9 Consulates in Lauterach/Bregenz, Graz, Innsbruck and Salzburg

Austrian Institute 28 Rutland Gate,

London SW7 1PQ ✆ 0171-584 8653

Electricity 220 volts AC

Currency Austrian Schilling (Sch) divided into 100 Groschen. Approx Sch17 to £1.

Time End September-end March: GMT +1 hour; end March-end September: GMT +2 hours

Travel Freedom Pass allows 3, 5 or 10 days unlimited travel in 1 month on the railways of Austria. Cost from £61 (under 26) or £76 (26+). Available from British Rail International Rail Centre, Victoria Station, London SW1V 1JY ✆ 0171-834 2345.

The following companies can arrange low-cost flights to Austria, and may also be able to help with Eurotrain/Inter-Rail passes, internal travel, insurance and tours:

Anglo-Austrian Society, 46 Queen's Gate, London SW1H 9AU ✆ 0171-222 0366.

Campus Travel, offices throughout the UK including a student travel centre at 52 Grosvenor Gardens, London SW1W 0AG ✆ 0171-730 3402 or ✆ 0131-668 3303 for Scottish telephone bookings.

Council Travel, 28A Poland Street, London W1V 3DB ✆ 0171-287 3337 (offices also in Paris, Nice, Lyon, Munich, Düsseldorf, Tokyo, Singapore and throughout the US).

Useful publications The Vienna Tourist Board publish a *Youth Scene* magazine which gives plenty of useful information for young visitors to the city. Available from the Vienna Tourist Board, 1025 Vienna or from the Austrian National Tourist Office, see above.

Entry regulations Holders of British and Irish passports and nationals of most European and many overseas countries need no visa to enter Austria, although visas may still be required by nationals of some Commonwealth countries. Further information and application forms are available from Austrian Consulates.

BALTIC STATES

Estonian Embassy 16 Hyde Park Gate, Kensington, London SW7 5DG
℗ 0171-589 7212-5

British Embassy Kentmanni 20, Talinn 200001, Estonia ℗ (372) 455328/9

Latvian Embassy 72 Queensborough Terrace, London W2 3SP ℗ 0171-727 1698

British Embassy 3rd Floor, Elizabetes Iela 2, 226010 Riga, Latvia ℗ (371) 320 737

Lithuanian Embassy 17 Essex Villas, London W8 7BP ℗ 0171-938 2481

British Embassy 2 Anakalnio, Gatve, PO Box 863, 2055 Vilnius, Lithuania
℗ (370) 22 20 70/1

Electricity 220 volts AC (50 cycles)

Currency Estonia: the Kroon (EEK), divided into 100 sents; approx EEK22 to £1. Latvia: the Lat, divided into 100 santimi; approx Lat 0.86 to £1. Lithuania: the Litas (LT); approx LT6 to £1.

Time GMT + 2 hours

Travel The following companies can arrange low-cost flights to Estonia, Latvia and Lithuania, and may also be able to help with internal travel, insurance and tours:

Finlandia Travel Ltd, 227 Regent Street, London W1R 7DB ℗ 0171-409 7334.

Campus Travel, offices throughout the UK including a student travel centre at 52 Grosvenor Gardens, London SW1W 0AG ℗ 0171-730 2101 or ℗ 0131-668 3303 for Scottish telephone bookings.

Council Travel, 28A Poland Street, London W1V 3DB ℗ 0171-437 7767 (offices also in Paris, Nice, Lyon, Munich, Düsseldorf, Tokyo, Singapore and throughout the US).

Entry regulations UK nationals require a valid full passport, but there is no visa requirement for stays of up to 30 days. Other nationalities should check requirements with embassies.

Useful publications Lonely Planet's *Baltic States & Kaliningrad - A Travel Survival Kit* £9.95 offers practical, down-to-earth information for budget travellers wanting to explore beyond the usual tourist routes.

Bed & breakfast/Farm accommodation The Latvian International Tourism Association, Lauku Celotajs (Country Traveller), Repúblikás Square 2-1120, Riga, LV-1981, Latvia ℗ (371 2) 327629 Fax (371 2) 325433 or (371 8) 830041 is a non-profit organisation offering a wide variety of individual travel packages, farm holidays, bed & breakfast accommodation and tailor-made group tours.

BELGIUM

Belgian Embassy 103-105 Eaton Square, London SW1W 9AB ℗ 0171-235 5422

Belgian National Tourist Office Premier House, 2 Gayton Road, Harrow, Middlesex HA1 2XU ℗ 0181-861 3300

British Embassy Rue d'Arlon 85, 1040 Brussels ℗ (32 2) 287 6211
Consulates in Antwerp and Liège

British Tourist Authority 306 Avenue Louise, 1050 Brussels ℗ (32 2) 646 3510 Fax (32 2) 646 3986

Electricity 220 volts AC

Currency Belgian Franc (BF), divided into 100 centimes. Approximately BF50 to £1.

Time End September-end March: GMT +1 hour; end March-end September: GMT +2 hours

Travel Belgian National Railways, 10 Greycoat Place, London SW1P 1SB ℗ 0891 516444 (calls charged at 35p/45p per minute) operates a scheme whereby a bike can be hired at one of 35 Belgian stations. Advisable to reserve in advance. Cost approx £5 per day, £3 for rail ticket holders.

The Benelux Tourrail Card entitles the holder to 5 days unlimited travel within a specified period of 1 month on the national rail networks of Belgium, Luxembourg and the Netherlands. Cost from £60 (under 26) or from £80 (26+). Details from Netherlands Railways, 25/28 Buckingham Gate, London SW1E 6LD ✆ 0171-630 1735.

Freedom Pass allows 3, 5 or 10 days unlimited rail travel in 1 month on Belgian railways. Cost from £31 (under 26) or from £38 (26+). Available from British Rail International Rail Centre, Victoria Station, London SW1V 1JY ✆ 0171-834 2345.

The following companies can arrange low-cost flights to Belgium, and may also be able to help with Eurotrain/Inter-Rail passes, internal travel, insurance and tours:

Campus Travel, offices throughout the UK including a student travel centre at 52 Grosvenor Gardens, London SW1V 1JY ✆ 0171-730 3402 or ✆ 0131-668 3303 for Scottish telephone bookings.

Council Travel, 28A Poland Street, London W1V 3DB ✆ 0171-287 3337 (offices also in Paris, Nice, Lyon, Munich, Düsseldorf, Tokyo, Singapore and throughout the US).

Entry regulations EU nationals and nationals of most Commonwealth countries do not require a visa for visits of up to 3 months. Visas may be necessary for citizens of certain Commonwealth countries. Further information and application forms from visa sections of Belgian embassies.

Useful publications *The Rough Guide to Holland, Belgium and Luxembourg* £9.99 provides comprehensive background information, with details on getting there, getting around and places to explore.

Bed & breakfast/Farm accommodation The Belgian National Tourist Office, see above, publishes a *Budget Holidays* brochure which lists farms offering accommodation (early booking advised) and has addresses of organisations offering bed & breakfast accommodation.

Windrose, Chambre d' Amis, Avenue Paul Dejaer 21A, 1060 Brussels ✆ (32 2) 534 7191 Fax (32 2) 534 7192 can arrange bed & breakfast accommodation throughout Belgium. Prices from BF1,000 per night.

Taxistop, Onderbergen 51, 9000 Gent ✆ (32 9) 223 2310 Fax (32 9) 224 3144 publishes an annual bed & breakfast guide covering Belgium, Luxembourg and the Netherlands, cost BF100.

BRAZIL

Brazilian Embassy 32 Green Street, Mayfair, London W1Y 4AT ✆ 0171-499 0877

British Embassy Avenida das Naçoes, Caixa Postal 07-0586, 70.359 Brasilia, DF, Brazil ✆ (55 61) 225 2710 Consulates in Belém, Manáus, Rio de Janeiro, Belo Horizonte, Fortaleza, Recife, Salvador, Sao Paulo, Porto Alegre, Rio Grande, Santos and Curitiba.

Electricity 110 volts AC/220 volts AC

Currency The Real (Rl); approx Rl 1.4 to £1

Health Travellers are advised to take precautions against cholera, typhoid, malaria and hepatitis.

Time GMT -3 hours

Travel The following companies can arrange low-cost flights to Brazil, and may also be able to help with internal travel, insurance and tours:

Campus Travel, offices throughout the UK, including a student travel centre at 52 Grosvenor Gardens, London SW1W 0AG ✆ 0171-730 8111 or ✆ 0131-668 3303 for Scottish telephone bookings.

Council Travel, 28A Poland Street, London WIV 3DB ℂ 0171-437 7767 (offices also in Paris, Nice, Lyon, Munich, Düsseldorf, Tokyo, Singapore and throughout the US).

North-South Travel, Moulsham Mill, Parkway, Chelmsford CM2 7PX ℂ Chelmsford (01245) 492882. All profits given to projects in the developing world.

STA Travel, 86 Old Brompton Road, London SW7 3LQ/117 Euston Road, London NW1 2SX ℂ 0171-937 9962 (offices also in Birmingham, Bristol, Cambridge, Glasgow, Leeds, Manchester and Oxford).

Entry regulations UK nationals and nationals from most western European countries can obtain a 90 day tourist visa on entry into Brazil. French, Australian, New Zealand, Canadian and US nationals must obtain their visas in advance from Brazilian embassies in their home countries.

Useful publications *Brazil - A Travel Survival Kit* £10.95 provides comprehensive background information, with details on getting there, getting around and places to explore.

The Rough Guide to Brazil £7.95 provides comprehensive background information, with details on getting there, getting around and places to explore.

CANADA

Canadian High Commission Macdonald House, 1 Grosvenor Square, London W1X 0AB ℂ 0171-258 6600
Immigration Division: 38 Grosvenor Street, London W1X 0AA ℂ 0171-258 6601

Tourist Office Canada Tourism Program, Canadian High Commission, Canada House, Trafalgar Square, London SW1Y 5BJ ℂ 0171-258 6346

British High Commission 80 Elgin Street, Ottawa, Ontario K1P 5K7, Canada ℂ (1 613) 237 1530

Consulates in Halifax, Montreal, St John's, Toronto, Vancouver and Winnipeg

British Tourist Authority 111 Avenue Road, Suite 450, Toronto, Ontario M5R 3N8, Canada ℂ (1 416) 925 6326

Electricity 110 volts AC

Currency The Canadian dollar (Can$), divided into 100 cents. Approx Can$2.15 to £1.

Time GMT -3½ to -9 hours

Travel Canrailpass provides unlimited travel at a fixed cost over the entire rail network or over any of 3 designated territories. Cost from Can$220, 30 days nationwide. Greyhound Bus passes also available from £75 (7 days, low season). Details from Long-Haul Leisurail, PO Box 113, Bretton, Peterborough PE3 8HY ℂ Peterborough (01733) 335599.

Greyhound Lines of Canada offer unlimited travel passes for use on all their coach services. Prices start from £92 for 7 days. All tickets must be purchased before entering Canada. Details from Greyhound International, Sussex House, London Road, East Grinstead RH19 1LD ℂ East Grinstead (01342) 317317 Fax (01342) 328519, or from Long Haul Leisurail, see above.

The following companies can arrange low-cost flights to Canada, and may also be able to help with internal travel, insurance and tours:

Campus Travel, offices throughout the UK including a student travel centre at 52 Grosvenor Gardens, London SW1W 0AG ℂ 0171-730 2101 or ℂ 0131-668 3303 for Scottish telephone bookings.

Council Travel, 28A Poland Street, London WIV 3DB ℂ 0171-437 7767 (offices also in Paris, Nice, Lyon, Munich, Düsseldorf, Tokyo, Singapore and throughout the US).

North-South Travel, Moulsham Mill, Parkway, Chelmsford CM2 7PX ℂ Chelmsford

(01245) 492882. All profits given to projects in the developing world.

STA Travel, 86 Old Brompton Road, London SW7 3LQ/117 Euston Road, London NW1 2SX ✆ 0171-937 9971 (offices also in Birmingham, Bristol, Cambridge, Glasgow, Leeds, Manchester and Oxford).

Entry regulations Citizens of the UK and Ireland do not require a visa to enter Canada. Citizens of many other countries are also exempt, but as regulations may change they should contact the nearest Canadian diplomatic mission for more information.

Useful publications The Canadian Tourist Office, see above, publish an annual *Holiday Canada* guide which provides helpful practical hints covering health, climate and travel, and includes details of organisations handling reservations for bed and breakfast accommodation or who publish directories of homes participating in bed & breakfast schemes.

Travellers Survival Kit USA and Canada £9.95, is a down-to-earth, entertaining guide for travellers to North America. Describes how to cope with the inhabitants, officialdom and way of life in Canada and the US. Published by Vacation Work Publications, 9 Park End Street, Oxford, OX1 1HJ ✆ (01865) 241978.

Canada - A Travel Survival Kit £12.95, offers practical down-to-earth information for independent travellers wanting to explore beyond the usual tourist routes. Published by Lonely Planet and available from good bookshops.

The Rough Guide to Canada £10.99 provides comprehensive background information on Canada plus details on getting around, places to explore and cheap places to stay.

Culture Shock! Canada £6.95 introduces the reader to the people, customs, ceremonies, food and culture of Canada with checklists of dos and don'ts.

Bed & breakfast/Farm accommodation
A booking service for bed & breakfast accommodation throughout Canada is Capital Bed & Breakfast Reservation Service, 2071 Riverside Drive, Ottowa, Ontario K1H 7X2, Canada ✆ (1 613) 737 4129.

Most provinces, major towns and cities have bed & breakfast associations or registries, and guest farm or ranch accommodation is also available in some country areas; contact Canada Tourism Program or provincial tourist offices below for further details.

Alberta Tourism, Alberta House, 1 Mount Street, London W1Y 5AA ✆ 0171-491 3430 Fax 0171-499 1779

Tourism British Columbia, British Columbia House, 1 Regent Street, London SW1Y 4NS ✆ 0171-930 6857 Fax 0171-930 2012

Travel Manitoba, 7th Floor, 155 Carlton Street, Department 2055, Winnipeg, MB, Canada R3C 3H8 ✆ (1 204) 945 3777 Fax (1 204) 945 2302

New Brunswick Department of Economic Development & Tourism, PO Box 12345, Frederiction, NB, Canada E3B 5C3 ✆ (1 506) 453 2170 Fax (1 506) 453 7127

Newfoundland & Labrador Department of Tourism & Culture, PO Box 8730, St Johns, NF, Canada A1B 4J6 ✆ (1 709) 729 2830 Fax (1 709) 729 0057

Northwest Territories Department of Economic Development and Tourism, Yellowknife, Northwest Territories, Canada X1A 2L9 ✆ (1 403) 873 7200 Fax (1 403) 873 0294

Nova Scotia Tourism & Culture, PO Box 456, Halifax, NS, Canada B3J 2R5 ✆ (1 902) 424 4207 Fax (1 902) 424 2668

Ontario Travel, Queen's Park, Toronto, Ontario, Canada M7A 2E5 ✆ (1 416) 314 0944 Fax (1 416) 314 7372

Prince Edward Island Department of Tourism, Parks & Recreation, PO Box 940E,

Charlottetown, Prince Edward Island, Canada C1A 7MS ℂ (1 902) 368 4444/5555 Fax (1 902) 368 4438

Québec Tourism, Québec House, 59 Pall Mall, London SW1Y 5JH ℂ 0171-930 8314 Fax 0171-930 7938 24-hour brochure line ℂ 0171-930 9742

Tourism Saskatchewan, 1919 Saskatchewan Drive, Regina, Saskatchewan, Canada S4P 3V7 ℂ (1 306) 787 2300 Fax (1 306) 787 0715

Tourism Yukon, PO Box 2703, Whitehorse, Yukon, Canada Y1A 2C6 ℂ (1 403) 667 5340 Fax (1 403) 667 2634

CHILE

Chilean Embassy 12 Devonshire Street, London W1N 2DS ℂ 0171-580 6392

British Embassy Av El Bosque Norte 0125, Casilla 72-D or Casilla 16552, Santiago 9, Chile ℂ (56 2) 231 3737 Consulates in Antofagasta, Arica, Concepción, Punta Arenas and Valparaíso

Electricity 220 volts AC

Currency The peso ($), divided into 100 cents

Health Travellers are advised to take precautions against cholera, typhoid and malaria

Time GMT -4 hours

Travel The following companies can arrange low-cost flights to Chile, and may also be able to help with internal travel, insurance and tours:

Campus Travel, offices throughout the UK, including a student travel centre at 52 Grosvenor Gardens, London SW1W 0AG ℂ 0171-730 8111 or ℂ 0131-668 3303 for Scottish telephone bookings.

Council Travel, 28A Poland Street, London W1V 3DB ℂ 0171-437 7767 (offices also in Paris, Nice, Lyon, Munich, Düsseldorf, Tokyo, Singapore and throughout the US).

North-South Travel, Moulsham Mill, Parkway, Chelmsford CM2 7PX ℂ Chelmsford (01245) 492882. All profits given to projects in the developing world.

STA Travel, 86 Old Brompton Road, London SW7 3LQ/117 Euston Road, London NW1 2SX ℂ 0171-937 9962 (offices also in Birmingham, Bristol, Cambridge, Glasgow, Leeds, Manchester and Oxford).

Entry regulations Citizens of the UK and Ireland do not require a visa to enter Chile and stay for up to 90 days. Citizens of many other countries are also exempt, but should contact the visa section of the nearest Chilean embassy for further information.

Useful publications *Chile and Easter Island - A Travel Survival Kit* £9.95 offers practical, down-to-earth information for budget travellers wanting to explore beyond the usual tourist routes.

COSTA RICA

Costa Rican Embassy 2nd Floor, 36 Upper Brook Street, London W1Y 1PE ℂ 0171-495 3985 Consular Section: Flat 2, 38 Redcliffe Square, London SW10 9JY ℂ/Fax 0171-373 7973

British Embassy Apartado 815, Edificio Centro Colon, (11th Floor), San José 1007, Costa Rica ℂ (506) 21 55 66/21 57 16/21 58 16/55 29 37

Tourist Office Instituto Costarricense de Turismo, PO Box 777-1000, San José, Costa Rica ℂ (506) 22 1090 Fax (506) 23 5452

Electricity 110 volts AC

Currency The colón, divided into 100 céntimos

Health Travellers are advised to take precautions against malaria, typhoid and polio.

Time GMT -5 hours

Travel There are no direct flights to Costa Rica from the UK, but the following companies may be able to arrange low-cost flights via Miami, Amsterdam or other cities:

Campus Travel, offices throughout the UK including a student travel centre at 52 Grosvenor Gardens, London SW1W 0AG ✆ 0171-730 2101 or ✆ 0131-668 3303 for Scottish telephone bookings.

Council Travel, 28A Poland Street, London W1V 3DB ✆ 0171-437 7767 (offices also in Paris, Nice, Lyon, Munich, Düsseldorf, Tokyo, Singapore and throughout the US).

North-South Travel, Moulsham Mill, Parkway, Chelmsford CM2 7PX ✆ Chelmsford (01245) 492882. All profits given to projects in the developing world.

STA Travel, 86 Old Brompton Road, London SW7 3LQ/117 Euston Road, London NW1 2SX ✆ 0171-937 9971 (offices also in Birmingham, Bristol, Cambridge, Glasgow, Leeds, Manchester and Oxford).

Entry regulations UK and US nationals do not require visas for stays of up to 3 months. Other nationals should check requirements with diplomatic missions.

Useful publications Lonely Planet's *Costa Rica - A Travel Survival Kit* £8.95 offers practical, down-to-earth information for budget travellers wanting to explore beyond the usual tourist routes.

Bed & breakfast accommodation Bell's Home Hospitality, PO Box 185, 1000 San José, Costa Rica ✆ (506) 25 47 52 Fax (506) 24 58 84 can match travellers up with a compatible Costa Rican family; cost from US$45 per night including breakfast.

CZECH REPUBLIC & SLOVAKIA

Embassy of the Czech Republic 26-30 Kensington Palace Gardens, London W8 4QY ✆ 0171-243 1115 Fax 0171-727 9654 Visa section: 28 Kensington Palace Gardens, London W8 4QY ✆ 0171-243 7942/3

British Embassy Thunovská 14, 125 50 Prague, Czech Republic ✆ (42 2) 533347/8/9

Embassy of the Slovak Republic 25 Kensington Palace Gardens, W8 4QY ✆ 0171-243 0803 Fax 0171-727 5824

British Embassy Grösslingova 35, 811 09 Bratislava, Slovakia

Electricity 220 volts AC

Currency Czech Republic: the koruna ceskoslovenská (Kcs), divided into 100 hellers. Slovakia: the Slovenská koruna (SkK), divided into 100 haliers. Approx Kcs/SkK46-50 to £1.

Time End September-end March: GMT +1 hour; end March-end September: GMT +2 hours.

Travel Freedom Pass allows 3, 5 or 10 days travel on the railways of the Czech Republic or Slovakia. Cost for the Czech Republic from £30 (under 26) or from £39 (26+). Cost for Slovakia from £22 (under 26 or from £29 (26+). Available from British Rail International Rail Centre, Victoria Station, London SW1V 1JY ✆ 0171-834 2345

The following companies can arrange low-cost flights to the Czech Republic and Slovakia, and may also be able to help with Eurotrain/Inter-Rail passes, internal travel, insurance and tours:

Campus Travel, offices throughout the UK including a student travel centre at 52 Grosvenor Gardens, London SW1W 0AG ✆ 0171-730 3402 or ✆ 0131-668 3303 for Scottish telephone bookings.

Council Travel, 28A Poland Street, London WIV 3DB ✆ 0171-437 7767 (offices also in Paris, Nice, Lyon, Munich, Düsseldorf, Tokyo, Singapore and throughout the US).

STA Travel, 86 Old Brompton Road, London SW7 3LQ/117 Euston Road, London NW1 2SX ✆ 0171-937 9921 (offices also in Birmingham, Bristol, Cambridge, Glasgow, Leeds, Manchester and Oxford).

Entry regulations Visas are not required by UK nationals or nationals of most European countries. US nationals may stay for up to 30 days without a visa. Other nationals should check requirements with diplomatic missions.

Useful publications *The Rough Guide to the Czech and Slovak Republics* £8.99 and *The Rough Guide to Prague* £7.99 provide concise information on getting around and places to explore.

Lonely Planet's *Eastern Europe on a Shoestring* £13.95 provides practical information on budget travel in the Czech Republic and most other east European countries.

DENMARK

Royal Danish Embassy 55 Sloane Street, London SWIX 9SR ✆ 0171-333 0200 Fax 0171-333 0270

Danish Tourist Board 55 Sloane Street, London SWIX 9SR ✆ 0171-259 5959 *(open 11.00-16.00 hrs)*

British Embassy Kastelsvej 36/38/40, 2100 Copenhagen O ✆ (45) 35 26 46 00. Consulates in Aabenraa, Aalborg, Aarhus, Esbjerg, Fredericia, Herning, Odense and Ronne.

British Tourist Authority Montergade 3, 1116 Copenhagen K ✆ (45) 33 33 91 88

Electricity 220 volts AC

Currency The Danish Krone (DKr) divided into 100 Ore. Approx DKr9.60 to £1.

Time End September-end March: GMT +1 hour; end March-end September: GMT +2 hours.

Travel Freedom Pass allows 3, 5 or 10 days unlimited travel in 1 month on the railways of Denmark. Cost from £42 (under 26) or from £60 (26+). Available from British Rail International Rail Centre, Victoria Station, London ✆ 0171-834 2345

The ScanRail pass is a flexible rail pass for Scandinavia, valid for unlimited travel during 5 days within 15 days, 10 days within one month and one month consecutive. Cost from £94 (ages under 25) or from £125 (ages 25+) for 5 days. Discounts are offered on certain ferry and bus routes. Details from Norwegian State Railways, 21-24 Cockspur Street, London SW1Y 5DA ✆ 0171-930 6666.

The following companies can arrange low-cost flights to Denmark, and may also be able to help with internal travel, insurance and tours:

Campus Travel, offices throughout the UK including a student travel centre at 52 Grosvenor Gardens, London SW1W 0AG ✆ 0171-730 3402 or ✆ 0131-668 3303 for Scottish telephone bookings.

Council Travel, 28A Poland Street, London WIV 3DB ✆ 0171-287 3337 (offices also in Paris, Nice, Lyon, Munich, Düsseldorf, Tokyo, Singapore and throughout the US).

Entry regulations EU nationals do not require visas for stays of up to 3 months. Other nationals should check with Danish embassies.

Useful publications Lonely Planet's *Scandinavian and Baltic Europe on a Shoestring* £10.95 offers practical, down-to-earth information for the low budget independent traveller in Denmark and the Faroe Islands.

The Rough Guide to Scandinavia £10.99 provides comprehensive background information on Denmark and the Faroe Islands, with details on getting there, getting around, places to explore and cheap places to stay.

Michael's Guide to Scandinavia £10.95 is detailed and concise, providing invaluable practical advice for all kinds of travellers. Published by Inbal Travel.

All the above are available from good bookshops.

Maps and General Travel Information leaflet provides information on travel, customs and entry formalities, residence, the health service and other practical information. Available from the Danish Tourist Board, see above, price £2.50.

Farm accommodation A list of tour operators organising farm holidays is available from the Danish Tourist Board, *see above*. The following organisations also organise farm holidays across the country: Dansk Bonsegårdsferie, v/Horsens Turistbureau, Søndergade 26, 8700 Horsens ✆ (45) 75 62 38 22 Fax (45) 75 62 61 51 and Landsforeningen for Landboturisme, Låsbyvej 20, 8600 Skanderborg ✆ (45) 86 52 41 50 Fax (45) 86 52 13 50.

ECUADOR

Ecuadorian Embassy Flat 3b, 3 Hans Crescent, London SW1X 0LS ✆ 0171-584 1267

British Embassy Calle Gonzalez Suarez, 111 (Casilla 314), Quito, Ecuador ✆ (593 2) 560669

Electricity 110 volts AC

Currency The sucre (S), divided into 100 cents

Health Travellers are advised to take precautions against cholera, yellow fever, typhoid, polio and malaria

Time GMT -5 hours

Travel The following companies can arrange low-cost flights to Ecuador, and may also be able to help with internal travel, insurance and tours:

Campus Travel, offices throughout the UK, including a student travel centre at 52 Grosvenor Gardens, London SW1W 0AG ✆ 0171-730 8111 or ✆ 0131-668 3303 for Scottish telephone bookings.

Council Travel, 28 A Poland Street, London W1V 3DB ✆ 0171-437 7767 (offices also in Paris, Nice, Lyon, Munich, Düsseldorf, Tokyo, Singapore and throughout the US).

North-South Travel, Moulsham Mill, Parkway, Chelmsford CM2 7PX ✆ Chelmsford (01245) 492882. All profits are given to projects in the developing world.

STA Travel, 86 Old Brompton Road, London SW7 3LQ/117 Euston Road, London NW1 2SX ✆ 0171-937 9962 (offices also in Birmingham, Bristol, Cambridge, Glasgow, Leeds, Manchester and Oxford).

Entry regulations Citizens of any nationality, with the exception of China, North and South Korea, Vietnam and Cuba, do not require a visa to stay in Ecuador as tourists for up to 3 months.

Useful publications *Ecuador & the Galápagos Islands - A Travel Survival Kit* £10.95 offers practical, down-to-earth information for budget travellers wanting to explore beyond the usual tourist routes.

FINLAND

Finnish Embassy 38 Chesham Place, London SW1W 8HN ✆ 0171-235 9531 Fax 0171-235 3680

Finnish Tourist Board 66/68 Haymarket, London SW1Y 4RF ✆ 0171-839 4048 Fax 0171-321 0696

British Embassy Itainen Puistotie 17, 00140 Helsinki © (358 0) 661293 Consulates in Jyväskylä, Kotka, Kuopio, Mariehamn, Oulu, Pori, Tampere, Turku and Vaasa

Electricity 220 volts AC

Currency The markka (FM), divided into 100 pennies (p). Approx FM8 to £1.

Time End September-end March: GMT +1 hour; end March-end September: GMT +2 hours.

Travel Finnrailpass entitles the holder to unlimited travel on Finnish State Railways, cost from £63, 8 days. Available from Finlandia Travel, 223 Regent Street, London W1R 7DB © 0171-409 7334.

Freedom Pass allows 3, 5 or 10 days unlimited travel in 1 month on the railways of Denmark. Cost from £49 (under 26) or from £64 (26+). Available from British Rail International Rail Centre, Victoria Station, London © 0171-834 2345

The **ScanRail pass** is a flexible rail pass for Scandinavia, valid for unlimited travel during 5 days within 15 days, 10 days within one month and one month consecutive. Cost from £94 (ages under 25) or from £125 (ages 25+) for 5 days. Discounts are offered on certain ferry and bus routes. Details from Norwegian State Railways, 21-24 Cockspur Street, London SW1Y 5DA © 0171-930 6666.

The following companies can arrange low-cost flights to Finland, and may also be able to help with Eurotrain/Inter-Rail passes, internal travel, insurance and tours:

Campus Travel, offices throughout the UK including a student travel centre at 52 Grosvenor Gardens, London SW1W 0AG © 0171-730 3402 or © 0131-668 3303 for Scottish telephone bookings.

Council Travel, 28A Poland Street, London W1V 3DB © 0171-287 3337 (offices also in Paris, Nice, Lyon, Munich, Düsseldorf,

Tokyo, Singapore and throughout the US).

Entry regulations Scandinavians and citizens of Austria, Belgium, France, Germany, Liechtenstein, Luxembourg and Switzerland do not require visas for entry into Finland. EU nationals, as well as nationals of many other countries may stay for up to 3 months without a visa. All travellers should hold a return or onward ticket or other documents to next destination and show visible means of support.

Useful publications Lonely Planet's *Finland - A Travel Survival Kit* £9.95 and *Scandinavian and Baltic Europe on a Shoestring* £10.95 offer practical, down-to-earth information for the low-budget, independent traveller in Finland.

The Rough Guide to Scandinavia £10.99 provides comprehensive background information on getting around Finland, with details on getting there, getting around and places to explore.

Finland Facts and Map covers travel to and within Finland, accommodation, customs and other useful information. Available from the Finnish Tourist Board, see above.

Bed & breakfast accommodation The Finnish Tourist Board, see above, publish an annual *Budget Accommodation* guide which includes a list of bed and breakfast establishments. The Holiday Chain - Lomarengas issues a *Country Holidays* brochure giving details of over 100 locations; available from Lomarengas, Malminkaari 23c, 00700 Helsinki © (358 0) 3516 1321 Fax (358 0) 3516 1370. Prices range from FM80-FM195 per person per night.

Farm accommodation There are about 500 farms in Finland offering accommodation facilities. Details from the Holiday Chain - Lomarengas, see above, or from the Finnish 4H Federation, Abrahaminkatu 7, 00180 Helsinki © (358 0) 642 233 Fax (358 0) 642 274.

The Finnish Family Programme
Provides opportunities for native speakers of English, French or German to live as a member of a Finnish family whilst speaking their own language. Host families include both farming and urban or suburban families who may move into the country for the summer. Applicants are expected to help with household chores, and/or childcare. On farms the work also involves helping with milking, fruit picking and haymaking and gardening. Ages 18-23. 1-12 months, mostly June-August. Apply by 28 February for summer placements, or at least 3 months in advance for other times of the year. In the UK apply to the Central Bureau for Educational Visits and Exchanges, Seymour Mews, London W1H 9PE ✆ 0171-486 5101. Outside the UK, apply to the Centre for International Mobility, PB 343, 00531 Helsinki ✆ (358 0) 7747 7033.

FRANCE

French Embassy 58 Knightsbridge, London SW1X 7JT ✆ 0171-201 1000 Fax 0171-259 6498

Consular Section: 21 Cromwell Road, London SW7 2DQ ✆ 0171-838 2000 Fax 0171-838 2001

Visa Section: 6A Cromwell Place, London SW7 2EW ✆ 0891-200289 and 0171-838 2050 Fax 0171-838 2046

French Government Tourist Office 178 Piccadilly, London W1V 0AL ✆ 0891 244123

British Embassy 35 rue du Faubourg St Honoré, 75383 Paris Cedex 08 ✆ (33 1) 42 66 91 42. Consulates in Bordeaux, Biarritz, Boulogne, Calais, Cherbourg, Dunquerque, Le Havre, Lille, Lyon, Marseille, Nantes, Nice, St Malo-Dinard and Toulouse.

British Tourist Authority Tourisme de Grande-Bretagne, Maison de la Grande-Bretagne, 19 rue des Mathurins, 75009 Paris ✆ (33 1) 44 51 56 20 Fax (33 1) 44 51 56 21

Electricity 220 volts AC

Currency French Franc (FF) divided into 100 centimes. Approximately FF8.35 to £1.

Time End September-end March: GMT +1 hour; end March-end September: GMT +2 hours.

Travel Rent-a-Bike scheme available at 53 train stations, bookable in advance; FF1,500 deposit, cost FF55 per day, decreasing as the number of rental days increases. Carrisimo card available in France only for ages 12-25 offers up to 50% reduction on 4 or 8 journeys; valid 1 year. Holiday Return (Séjour) Ticket gives concession of 25% if the journey covers more than 1,000 km; valid 2 months. Further information from the Rail Shop ✆ 0891 515477 (calls cost 39p/49p per minute). For bookings call 0345 300 003.

Freedom Pass allows 3, 5 or 10 days unlimited rail travel in 1 month on the railways of France. Cost from £95 (under 26) or £114 (26+). Available from British Rail International Rail Centre, Victoria Station, London SW1V 1JY ✆ 0171-834 2345.

The following companies can arrange low-cost flights to France, and may also be able to help with Eurotrain/Inter-Rail passes, internal travel, insurance and tours:

Campus Travel, offices throughout the UK including a student travel centre at 52 Grosvenor Gardens, London SW1W 0AG ✆ 0171-730 3402 or ✆ 0131-668 3303 for Scottish telephone bookings.

Council Travel, 28A Poland Street, London W1V 3DB ✆ 0171-287 3337 (offices also in Paris, Nice, Lyon, Munich, Düsseldorf, Tokyo, Singapore and throughout the US).

STA Travel, 86 Old Brompton Road, London SW7 3LQ/117 Euston Road, London NW1 2SX ✆ 0171-937 9921 (offices also in Birmingham, Bristol, Cambridge, Glasgow, Leeds, Manchester and Oxford).

Entry regulations EU nationals and citizens of Andorra, Austria, Canada, Cyprus, Czech and Slovak Republics, Finland, Hungary, Iceland, Japan, Liechtenstein, Malta, Monaco, New Zealand, Norway, Poland, Singapore, Slovenia, South Korea, Sweden, Switzerland, US and Vatican do not require a visa for stays of up to 3 months. Other nationalities should contact their French Consulate for further information.

Useful publications *Rough Guides* provide comprehensive background information plus details on getting there, getting around and places to explore. Titles include *France* £9.99, *Paris* £7.99, *Brittany* and *Normandy* £7.99, *Provence and the Côte d'Azur* £8.99 and *Pyrénées* £7.99.

Lonely Planet's *France - A Travel Survival Kit* £13.95 offers practical, down-to-earth information for budget travellers wanting to explore beyond the usual tourist routes.

Culture Shock! France £6.95 introduces the reader to the people, customs, ceremonies, food and culture of France, with checklists of dos and don'ts.

Bed & breakfast accommodation Gîtes de France, 178 Piccadilly, London W1V 9DB ℂ 0171-493 3480 Fax 0171-495 6417 can provide details of bed & breakfast accommodation and a *Chambres d'Hôtes* scheme for those who wish to stay 2 or more nights in a French country home.

A guidebook *Café Couette* listing over 500 bed & breakfast accommodation addresses throughout France (including Paris) is available from the French Government Tourist Office, see above.

Bed et Breakfast à Lyon, 2 petite rue Tramassac, 69005 Lyon ℂ (33) 72 41 72 00 Fax (33) 72 41 76 66 can book bed and breakfast accommodation in France's second city.

GERMANY

Embassy of the Federal Republic of Germany 23 Belgrave Square, 1-6 Chesham Place, London SW1X 8PZ ℂ 0171-235 5033/0171-824 1300

German National Tourist Office Nightingale House, 65 Curzon Street, London W1Y 7PE ℂ 0171-495 3990

British Embassy Friedrich-Ebert Allee 77, 53113 Bonn ℂ (49 228) 23 40 61 and Unter den Linden 32/34, 1080 Berlin ℂ (49 30) 220 2431 Consulates in Bremen, Düsseldorf, Frankfurt/Main, Hamburg, Hanover, Kiel, Munich, Nuremberg and Stuttgart

British Tourist Authority Taunusstraße 52-60, 60329 Frankfurt ℂ (49 69) 23 80 711

Electricity 220 volts AC

Currency Deutschmark (DM) divided into 100 Pfennige. Approx DM2.50 to £1.

Time End September-end March: GMT +1 hour; end March-end September: GMT +2 hours.

Travel Freedom Pass allows 3, 5 or 10 days unlimited rail travel on the railways of Germany. Cost from £94 (under 26) or £125 (26+). Available from DER Travel Service, 18 Conduit Street, London W1R 9TD ℂ 0171-290 1116 or from British Rail International Rail Centre, Victoria Station, London SW1V 1JY ℂ 0171-834 2345

In larger cities there are agencies (*Mitfahrerzentrale*) which organise cost-sharing car travel to many parts of Germany and other European countries.

The following companies can arrange low-cost flights to Germany, and may also be able to help with Eurotrain/Inter-Rail passes, internal travel, insurance and tours:

Campus Travel, offices throughout the UK

including a student travel centre at 52 Grosvenor Gardens, London SW1W 0AG ✆ 0171-730 3402 or ✆ 0131-668 3303 for Scottish telephone bookings.

Council Travel, 28A Poland Street, London W1V 3DB ✆ 0171-287 3337 (offices also in Paris, Nice, Lyon, Munich, Düsseldorf, Tokyo, Singapore and throughout the US).

STA Travel, 86 Old Brompton Road, London SW7 3LQ/117 Euston Road, London NW1 2SX ✆ 0171-937 9921 (offices also in Birmingham, Bristol, Cambridge, Glasgow, Leeds, Manchester and Oxford).

Entry regulations EU nationals and citizens of Austria, Switzerland, Liechtenstein, Malta, Monaco, San Marino, United States, Canada, Japan, Australia, New Zealand, South Africa and a number of other countries do not require a visa for stays of up to 3 months.

Useful publications *Germany As You Like It* is a general folder with information on entry regulations, travel, accommodation and other facts for visitors. Available from the German National Tourist Office, *see above.*

The Rough Guide to Germany £11.99 and *The Rough Guide to Berlin* £8.99 provide comprehensive background information on Germany and its capital, plus details on getting there, getting around and places to explore.

Bed & breakfast accommodation The German National Tourist Office, see above, publishes an annual brochure listing some 500 towns and villages throughout Germany offering bed & breakfast accommodation.

Farm accommodation Information on farm holidays in Germany is available from the Deutsche Landwirtschaftsgesellschaft eV, Zimmerweg 16, 6000 Frankfurt/Main 1, Germany ✆ (49 69) 71 680 Fax (49 69) 724 1554.

GREAT BRITAIN

British Tourist Authority Thames Tower, Black's Road, Hammersmith, London W6 9EL ✆ 0181-846 9000. Offices in 19 countries and a network of information centres throughout Britain. Runs two British Travel Centres in London, at Victoria Station and at 12 Regent Street, open 7 days a week, and can book travel, reserve tours, change currency and provide information and advice.

Electricity 240 volts AC

Currency The pound Sterling (£), divided into 100 pence (p)

Time End October-end March: GMT; end March-end October: GMT +1 hour.

Travel Anyone under 24 or a full-time student in the UK can buy a British Rail Young Person's Railcard, entitling the holder to up to 33% off rail fares in Britain; cost £16 valid 1 year. Further details from principal British Rail stations or student travel offices. British Rail also offer a variety of discount tickets depending on age, time of day and distance to be travelled. Information from British Rail offices or agents outside Britain, and from any British Rail station.

National Express operate extensive coach services to most major towns and cities throughout the UK. Full-time students can buy a Coach Card entitling them to discounts on standard fares. Cost £7, valid 1 year. Further information from National Express ✆ 0181-770 7770.

Both the Young Persons Railcard and Coach Card are available from Campus Travel, who have offices throughout Britain, on university campuses, within YHA adventure shops and on the high street. London office is at 52 Grosvenor Gardens, London SW1W OAG ✆ 0171-730 3402.

Entry regulations EU nationals and citizens of most Commonwealth countries do not require a visa to enter Britain for holiday purposes. Commonwealth citizens and foreign nationals in doubt about their admission status can obtain entry certificates or letters of consent from their local British High Commission or Consular Office.

Bed & breakfast accommodation/Farm accommodation Bed and Breakfast (GB), PO Box 66, Bell Street, Henley-on-Thames RG9 IXS ✆ Henley-on-Thames (01491) 578803 Fax (01491) 410806 is a central booking agency for bed and breakfast accommodation in private homes and guest houses throughout Britain. Costs from £14-£45 per person per night, according to location and facilities offered. Reservations staff speak English, French and German. Car hire also available. **H**

The British Tourist Authority, see above, publish an annual guidebook *Stay in a British Home* which gives details of agencies and individuals offering family accommodation. Available free from British Tourist Authority offices overseas.

The Scottish Tourist Board, 23 Ravelston Terrace, Edinburgh EH4 3EU ✆ 0131-332 2433 publishes *Scotland Bed & Breakfast.* Price £5.80 including postage from the above address or from the STB's London office at 19 Cockspur Street, London SW1Y 5BL ✆ 0171-930 8661/2/3. Also available through British Tourist Authority offices abroad. Scottish *Farmhouse Holidays* brochure available from the STB or from the booking agent, Jane Buchanan, Drumtenant, Ladybank, Fife KY7 7UG ✆ Ladybank (01337) 30451.

The Wales Tourist Board, Brunel House, Fitzalan Road, Cardiff CF2 IUY ✆ Cardiff (01222) 499909 publish a free annual brochure listing approved farmhouse accommodation; also a selection of leaflets listing farm holiday addresses by region.

The Farm Holiday Bureau, National Agricultural Centre, Stoneleigh Park, Warwickshire CV8 21 Z ✆ Coventry (01203) 696909 Fax (01203) 696630 publish *Stay on a Farm,*

listing over 1,000 farmhouse bed and breakfast orself catering establishments throughout Britain. Available from bookshops, price £5.95, or direct from the Farm Holiday Bureau, price £7.50.

GREECE

Greek Embassy 1A Holland Park, London W11 3TP ✆ 0171-221 6467 Fax 0171-229 7221

National Tourist Organisation of Greece 4 Conduit Street, London W1R 0DI ✆ 0171-734 5997

British Embassy 1 Ploutarchou Street, 106 75 Athens ✆ (30 1) 7236 211 Consulates in Corfu, Crete, Patras, Rhodes, Salonika and Syros

Electricity 220 volts AC

Currency The drachma (Dr). Approx Dr370 to £1

Time End September-end March: GMT +2 hours; end March-end September: GMT +3 hours.

Travel Freedom Pass allows 3, 5 or 10 days unlimited rail travel in one month on the railways of Greece. Cost from £34 (under 26) or £44 (26+). Available from British Rail International Rail Centre, Victoria Station, London SW1V IJY ✆ 0171-834 2345.

The following companies can arrange low-cost flights to Greece, and may also be able to help with Eurotrain/Inter-Rail passes, internal travel, insurance and tours:

Campus Travel, offices throughout the UK including a student travel centre at 52 Grosvenor Gardens, London SW1W 0AG ✆ 0171-730 3402 or ✆ 0131-668 3303 for Scottish telephone bookings.

Council Travel, 28A Poland Street, London W1V 3DB ✆ 0171-287 3337 (offices also in Paris, Nice, Lyon, Munich, Düsseldorf,

Tokyo, Singapore and throughout the US).

STA Travel, 86 Old Brompton Road, London SW7 3LQ/117 Euston Road, London NW1 2SX © 0171-937 9921 (offices also in Birmingham Bristol, Cambridge, Glasgow, Leeds, Manchester and Oxford).

Entry regulations EU nationals and nationals of Australia do not require a visa for stays of up to 3 months. All other nationalities should check visa requirements with Greek embassies.

Useful publications *The Rough Guide to Greece* £9.99 and *The Rough Guide to Crete* £6.99 provide comprehensive background information, plus details getting there, getting around and places to explore.

Lonely Planet's *Greece - A Travel Survival Kit* £10.95 offers practical, down-to-earth information for the independent traveller wanting to explore beyond the usual tourist routes.

HONG KONG

Hong Kong Government Immigration Division 7 Gloucester Road, Wanchai, Hong Kong © (852) 829 3283

Hong Kong Tourist Association 125 Pall Mall, London SW1Y 5EA © 0171-930 4775

Electricity 200 volts AC

Currency The Hong Kong dollar (HK$), divided into 100 cents. Approx HK$12 to £1.

Health Travellers are advised to take precautions against cholera and typhoid

Time GMT + 8 hours

Travel The following companies can arrange low-cost flights to Hong Kong, and may also be able to help with internal travel, insurance and tours:

Campus Travel, offices throughout the UK including a student travel centre at 52 Grosvenor Gardens, London SW1W 0AG © 0171-730 8111 or © 0131-668 3303 for Scottish telephone bookings.

Council Travel, 28A Poland Street, London W1V 3DB © 0171-437 7767 (offices also in Paris, Nice, Lyon, Munich, Düsseldorf, Tokyo, Singapore and throughout the US).

North-South Travel, Moulsham Mill, Parkway, Chelmsford CM2 7PX © Chelmsford (01245) 492882. All profits given to projects in the developing world.

STA Travel , 86 Old Brompton Road, London SW8 3LQ/117 Euston Road, London NW1 2SX © 0171-937 9962 (offices also in Birmingham, Bristol, Cambridge, Glasgow, Leeds, Manchester and Oxford).

Entry regulations British citizens may stay for up to 6 months without a visa. For citizens of other countries visa-free stays of between 1-3 months may be allowed, depending on the country; they should check their status at any British Consulate, Visa Office or High Commission before departure.

Useful publications *The Rough Guide to Hong Kong and Macau* £8.99 provides comprehensive background information and details on getting there, getting around and places to explore.

Lonely Planet's *Hong Kong, Macau & Canton - A Travel Survival Kit* £8.95 offers practical, down to earth information for budget travellers.

Bed & breakfast accommodation
Bed & Breakfast Homestays Hong Kong, GPO Box 8947, Central, Hong Kong © (852) 849 8485 Fax (852) 813 1059 can arrange accommodation with host families in many areas of Hong Kong. Minimum stay 2 nights; cost from £38.

HUNGARY

Hungarian Embassy 35 Eaton Place, London SW1X 8BV © 071-235 4048/7179 Visa section: © 0171-235 2664

Hungarian Tourist Board 6 Conduit Street, London W1R 9TG © 0171-491 3588

British Embassy Harmincad Utca 6, Budapest V, Hungary © (36 1) 266 2888

Electricity 220 volts AC

Currency The forint (Ft), divided into 100 fillér

Time End September-end March: GMT +1 hour; end March-end September: GMT +2 hours.

Travel Freedom Pass allows 3, 5 or 10 days travel in one month on the railways of Hungary. Cost from £29 (under 26) or £36 (26+). Available from British Rail International Rail Centre, Victoria Station, London SW1V 1JY © 0171-834 2345.

The following companies can arrange low-cost flights to Hungary, and may also be able to help with Eurotrain/Inter-Rail passes, internal travel, insurance and tours:

Campus Travel, offices throughout the UK including a student travel centre at 52 Grosvenor Gardens, London SW1W 0AG © 0171-730 3402 or © 0131-668 3303 for Scottish telephone bookings.

Council Travel 28A Poland Street, London W1V 3DB © 0171-437 7767 (offices also in Paris, Nice, Lyon, Munich, Düsseldorf, Tokyo, Singapore and throughout the US).

Entry regulations Entry visas are not required for British/Irish passport holders, most European nationals and Americans; however travellers must hold a full 10 year passport.

Useful publications *The Rough Guide to Hungary* £7.99 provides comprehensive background information, with details on getting there, getting around and places to explore.

Lonely Planet's *Hungary - A Travel Survival Kit* £9.95 offers practical, down-to-earth information for the independent traveller wanting to explore beyond the usual tourist routes. Also *Eastern Europe on a Shoestring* £13.95, a handbook for budget travellers.

Michael's Guide to Hungary £6.95 is detailed and concise providing invaluable practical advice for all kinds of traveller. Published by Inbal Travel.

INDIA

India High Commission India House, Aldwych, London WC2B 4NA © 0171-836 8484

Government of India Tourist Office 7 Cork Street, London W1X 1PB © 0171-437 3677

British High Commission Chanakyapuri, New Delhi 1100-21, India © (91 11) 601371. Deputy High Commission offices in Bombay, Calcutta and Madras.

Electricity 220 volts AC; some areas also have DC supplies

Currency The Rupee (R) divided into 100 Paise. Approx Rs48 to £1.

Health Travellers are advised to take precautions against cholera, typhoid and malaria, and a certificate of inoculation against yellow fever is required if they have travelled from or through an infected area

Time GMT +5½ hours

Travel SD Enterprises Ltd, 103 Wembley Park Drive, Wembley, Middlesex HA9 0PA © 0181-903 3411 issues the Indrail Pass which allows unlimited travel on all trains throughout India, with no charge for night sleepers or reservations. Available for periods of 1, 7, 15, 21, 30, 60 or 90 days. Cost from $15. Also available from Campus Travel, see below, or the Government of India Tourist Office, see above.

Indian Airlines operates a youth fare scheme entitling those aged 12-30 to a discount of 25% off the normal fare, all year. Also Discover India scheme offering unlimited air travel within India. 21 days, all year, cost $400. Further information from the Government of India Tourist Office, see above.

The following companies can arrange low-cost flights to India, and may also be able to help with internal travel, insurance and tours:

Campus Travel, offices throughout the UK, including a student travel centre at 52 Grosvenor Gardens, London SW1W 0AG ℭ 0171-730 8111 or ℭ 0131-668 3303 for Scottish telephone bookings.

Council Travel, 28A Poland Street, London W1V 3DB ℭ 0171-287 3337 (offices also in Paris, Nice, Lyon, Munich, Düsseldorf, Tokyo, Singapore and throughout the US).

North-South Travel, Moulsham Mill, Parkway, Chelmsford CM2 7PX ℭ Chelmsford (01245) 492882. All profits are given to projects in the developing world.

STA Travel, 86 Old Brompton Road, London SW7 3LQ ℭ 0171-937 9962 (offices also in Birmingham, Bristol, Cambridge, Glasgow, Leeds, Manchester and Oxford).

Trailfinders Travel Centre, 42-50 Earls Court Road, London W8 6EJ ℭ 0171-938 3366 and Trailfinders, 194 Kensington High Street, London W8 7RG ℭ 0171-938 3939 (also branches in Bristol, Glasgow and Manchester).

Entry regulations All nationals require a visa to enter India. For visa application forms contact your local travel agent or Indian High Commission/Embassy.

Useful publications *Travel Information* provides information on accommodation, currency, climate, customs, health/entry regulations, inland travel and languages in India. Available from the Government of India Tourist Office, see above.

Lonely Planet's *India - A Travel Survival Kit* £14.95 offers practical, down-to-earth information for low-budget travellers wanting to explore beyond the usual tourist routes.

Culture Shock! India £6.95 is a guide written for international travellers of any background. The reader is introduced to the people, customs, ceremonies, food and culture of India, with checklists of dos and dont's.

INDONESIA

Indonesian Embassy 38 Grosvenor Square, London W1X 9AD ℭ 0171-499 7661 Consular Department: 61 Welbeck Street, London W1M 7HB ℭ 0171-499 7661

British Embassy Jalan M H Thamrin 75, Jakarta 10310, Indonesia ℭ (62) 21 330904 Consulates in Medan and Surabaya

Electricity 220 volts AC is usual although 110 volts still in use

Currency The rupiah (Rp) divided into 100 sen

Health Travellers are advised to take precautions against malaria, cholera, typhoid and polio, and certificates of inoculation against cholera and yellow fever are required if they have travelled from or through an infected area

Time GMT +7-9 hours

Travel The following companies can arrange low-cost flights to Indonesia, and may also be able to help with internal travel, insurance and tours:

Campus Travel, offices throughout the UK, including a student travel centre at 52 Grosvenor Gardens, London SW1W 0AG ✆ 0171-730 8111 or ✆ 0131-668 3303 for Scottish telephone bookings.

Council Travel, 28A Poland Street, London W1V 3DB ✆ 0171-287 3337 (offices also in Paris, Nice, Lyon, Munich, Düsseldorf, Tokyo, Singapore and throughout the US).

North-South Travel, Moulsham Mill, Parkway, Chelmsford CM2 7PX ✆ Chelmsford (01245) 492882. All profits are given to projects in the developing world.

STA Travel, 86 Old Brompton Road, London SW7 3LQ ✆ 0171-937 9962 (offices also in Birmingham, Bristol, Cambridge, Glasgow, Leeds, Manchester and Oxford).

Trailfinders Travel Centre, 42-50 Earls Court Road, London W8 6EJ ✆ 0171-938 3366 and Trailfinders, 194 Kensington High Street, London W8 7RG ✆ 0171-938 3939 (also branches in Bristol, Glasgow and Manchester).

Entry regulations For stays of up to 2 months visas are not required for UK and EU nationals, nor for nationals of Australia, Austria, Brazil, Canada, Chile, Finland, Iceland, Japan, Malaysia, Malta, Mexico, Morocco, New Zealand, Norway, the Philippines, Singapore, South Korea, Sweden, Switzerland, Thailand, the US and Venezuela.

Useful publications Lonely Planet's *Indonesia - A Travel Survival Kit* £14.95 offers practical, down-to-earth information for budget travellers wanting to explore beyond the usual tourist routes.

IRELAND

Irish Embassy 17 Grosvenor Place, London SW1X 7HR ✆ 0171-235 2171

Irish Tourist Board Ireland House, 150-151 New Bond Street, London W1Y 0AQ ✆ 0171-493 3201

British Embassy 31/33 Merrion Road, Dublin 4 ✆ (353 1) 269 5211

British Tourist Authority 123 Lower Baggot Street, Dublin 2 ✆ (353 1) 661 4188

Electricity 230 volts AC

Currency The Irish Pound (IR£), divided into 100 pence. Approx IR£1 to £1.

Time End October-end March: GMT; end March-end October: GMT +1 hour.

Travel Freedom Pass allows 3, 5 or 10 days unlimited travel in 1 month on the railways of Ireland. Cost from £36 (under 26) or £38 (26+). Available from British Rail International Rail Centre, Victoria Station, London SW1V 1JY ✆ 0171-834 2345.

The following companies can arrange low-cost flights to Ireland, and may also be able to help with Eurotrain/Inter-Rail passes, ferries, internal travel, insurance and tours:

Campus Travel, offices throughout the UK, including a student travel centre at 52 Grosvenor Gardens, London SW1W 0AG ✆ 0171-730 3402 or ✆ 0131-668 3303 for Scottish telephone bookings

Council Travel, 28A Poland Street, London W1V 3DB ✆ 0171-287 3337 (offices also in Paris, Nice, Lyon, Munich, Düsseldorf, Singapore, Tokyo and throughout the US).

Entry regulations Passports are not required by British citizens born in the United Kingdom travelling from Britain. Those resident in Britain but not holding a British passport who intend to holiday in Ireland may require a passport and a visa. Information concerning those nationals who require a visa can be obtained from the Irish Embassy, see above.

Useful publications *The Rough Guide to Ireland* £9.99 provides comprehensive background information, with details on getting there, getting around and places to explore.

Lonely Planet's *Ireland - A Travel Survival Kit* £11.95 offers practical, down-to-earth information for budget travellers wanting to explore beyond the usual tourist routes.

Bed & breakfast/Farm accommodation

There is a large amount of privately-run home and farmhouse accommodation in Ireland. Tourist information offices can provide lists of local family homes offering accommodation, which will all have been inspected and approved by the Irish Tourist Board. This type of accommodation costs between IR£13-IR£16 per person per night. A list of tourist information offices in Ireland is available from the Irish Tourist Board, see above.

The Town & Country Homes Association, Donegal Road, Ballyshannon, Co Donegal © (353 72) 51377 Fax (353 72) 51207 publishes an annual illustrated brochure, price IR£2.50 listing homes throughout Ireland, approved by the Irish Tourist Board.

Irish Country Holidays, Bord na Mona House, 76 Lower Baggot Street, Dublin 2 © (353 1) 688 555 ext 131 Fax (353 1) 601800 is a grouping of local communities spread across Ireland who offer guests a chance to live as part of a community and share in their pastimes, customs and entertainments, including daily farming and rural activities.

The Irish Farm Holiday Association, Glynch House New Bliss, Co Monaghan © (353 47) 53421 publishes an annual illustrated guidebook, price £3 (Sterling) listing farmhouses throughout the country offering hospitality.

ISRAEL

Israeli Embassy 2 Palace Green, Kensington, London W8 4QB © 0171-957 9500

Israel Government Tourist Office

18 Great Marlborough Street, London W1V 1AF © 0171-434 3651

British Embassy 192 Hayarkon Street, Tel Aviv 63405 © (972 3) 524 9171/8 Consulates in Eilat and Tel Aviv

Electricity 220 volts AC

Currency The New Israeli Shequel (NIS), divided into 100 agorot

Health Travellers are advised to take precautions against typhoid

Time End August-end March: GMT +2 hours; end March-end August: GMT +3 hours

Travel The following companies can arrange low-cost flights to Israel, and may also be able to help with internal travel, insurance and tours:

Campus Travel, offices throughout the UK including a student travel centre at 52 Grosvenor Gardens, London SW1W 0AG © 0171-730 3402 or © 0131-668 3303 for Scottish telephone bookings.

Council Travel, 28A Poland Street, London W1V 3DB © 0171-287 3337 (offices also in Paris, Nice, Lyon, Munich, Düsseldorf, Tokyo, Singapore and throughout the US).

North-South Travel, Moulsham Mill, Parkway, Chelmsford CM2 7PX © Chelmsford (01245) 492882. All profits given to projects in the developing world.

STA Travel, 86 Old Brompton Road, London SW7 3LQ © 0171-937 9921 (offices also in Birmingham, Bristol, Cambridge, Glasgow, Leeds, Manchester and Oxford).

Entry regulations British passport holders require no visa for a tourist visit to Israel. Other nationalities should contact Israeli embassies for details of visa requirements.

Useful publications Lonely Planet's *Israel - A Travel Survival Kit* £10.95 offers practical, down-to-earth information for budget travellers wanting to explore beyond the usual tourist routes.

Culture Shock! Israel £6.95 introduces the reader to the people, customs, ceremonies, food and culture of Israel with checklists of dos and don'ts.

Contacts The Israeli Ministry of Tourism run a Meet the Israeli scheme. Guests are invited into the home of an Israeli family to spend an afternoon or evening and to have a chat over a cup of tea or coffee. Guests may request to meet members of a particular trade or profession. Such home hospitality requests may be arranged at any Tourist Information Office in Israel; details from the Israel Government Tourist Office, see above.

The Israel Government Tourist Office also issues a list of addresses offering bed & breakfast accommodation, many of them being moshavim. These are collectives of individual smallholders, based on the family unit. Each family works and develops its own plot of land or farm while sharing the capital costs of equipment and marketing. Moshavim also accept volunteers who live and work as members of the family and are expected to share in the social and cultural activities of the community. Most of the work is on the land, with emphasis on flower growing, market gardening and specialist fruit farming. Details of organisations recruiting moshav volunteers are given in *Working Holidays*, the Central Bureau's annual international guide to seasonal job opportunities.

ITALY

Italian Embassy 14 Three Kings Yard, Davies Street, London W1Y 2EH ✆ 0171-312 2200

Italian State Tourist Board (ENIT) 1 Princes Street, London W1R 8AY ✆ 0171-408 1254

British Embassy Via XX Settembre 80A, 00187 Rome ✆ (39 6) 482 5441/5551 Consulates in Bari, Brindisi, Florence, Genoa, Milan, Naples, Turin, Trieste and Venice

British Tourist Authority Corso Vittorio Emanuele 337, 00186 Rome ✆ (29 6) 6880 6464

Electricity 220 volts AC

Currency The Italian Lira, plural Lire (L). Approx L2430 to £1.

Time End September - end March: GMT + 1 hour; end March - end September: GMT +2 hours

Travel CIT (England) Ltd, 3-5 Lansdowne Road, Croydon, Surrey CR9 1LL ✆ 0181-686 0677 issues a Kilometric ticket valid for 3,000km (maximum 20 journeys) which can be shared by up to 5 people, 3,000km being divided by the number of passengers. Valid 2 months, cost £90. Travel at Will ticket entitles the holder to unlimited travel on the Italian rail network from £88 (8 consecutive days).

Freedom Pass allows 3, 5 or 10 days unlimited rail travel in 1 month on the railways of Italy. Cost from £79 (under 26) or £105 (26+) for 3 days. Available from British Rail International Rail Centre, Victoria Station, London SW1Y 1JY ✆ 0171-834 2345.

The following companies can arrange low-cost flights to Italy, and may also be able to help with Eurotrain/Inter-Rail passes, internal travel, insurance and tours:

Campus Travel, offices throughout the UK including a student travel centre at 52 Grosvenor Gardens, London SW1W 0AG ✆ 0171-730 3402 or ✆ 0131-668 3303 for Scottish telephone bookings.

Council Travel, 28A Poland Street, London W1V 3DB ✆ 0171 287 3337 (offices also in Paris, Nice, Lyon, Munich, Düsseldorf, Tokyo, Singapore and throughout the US).

STA Travel, 86 Old Brompton Road, London SW7 3LQ/117 Euston Road, London NW1 2SX ✆ 0171-937 9921 (offices also in Birmingham, Bristol, Cambridge, Glasgow, Leeds, Manchester and Oxford).

Entry regulations EU nationals may stay for up to 3 months without a visa, other nationals should check with the Italian embassy in their country.

Useful publications *Italy, Travellers Handbook is* a free booklet containing useful information for visitors with notes on accommodation, culture and leisure, sports and travel. Also includes general information, and the addresses of provincial and local tourist boards. Available from the Italian State Tourist Board, *see above.*

Lonely Planet's *Italy - A Travel Survival Kit* £11.95 offers practical, down-to-earth information for budget travellers wanting to explore beyond the usual tourist routes.

Rough Guides provide comprehensive background information with details on getting around and places to explore. Titles include *Italy* £12.99, *Sicily* £8.99, *Tuscany & Umbria* £8.99 and *Venice* £8.99

JAPAN

Japanese Embassy 101/104 Piccadilly, London W1V 9FN ℂ 0171-465 6500

Japan National Tourist Organisation 167 Regent Street, London W1R 7FD ℂ 0171-734 9638

British Embassy No 1 Ichiban-cho, Chiyoda-ku, Tokyo 102 ℂ (81 3) 3265 6340 Consulates in Fukuoka, Hiroshima, Nagoya and Osaka

British Tourist Authority Tokyo Club Building, 3-2-6 Kasumigaseki, Chiyoda-ku, Tokyo 100 ℂ Tokyo (81 3) 3581 3603/4 Fax (81 3) 3581 5797

Electricity 100 volts AC; 2 different cycles in use: 50 in eastern Japan (including Tokyo) 60 in western Japan (including Nagoya, Kyoto and Osaka)

Currency The yen (¥) approximately ¥150 to £1

Health Travellers are advised to take precautions against cholera and typhoid.

Time GMT +9 hours.

Travel The Japan Rail Pass provides first class or economy travel passes throughout the Japanese rail network. Available for 7,14 or 21 days; cost from £172, economy. Details from Long-Haul Leisurail, PO Box 113, Bretton, Peterborough PE3 8HY ℂ Peterborough (01733) 335599.

The following companies can arrange low-cost flights to Japan, and may also be able to help with internal travel, insurance and tours:

Campus Travel, offices throughout the UK including a student travel centre at 52 Grosvenor Gardens, London SW1V 0AG ℂ 0171-730 8111 or ℂ 0131-668 3303 for Scottish telephone bookings.

Council Travel, 28A Poland Street, London W1V 3DB ℂ 0171-437 7767 (offices also in Paris, Nice, Lyon, Munich, Düsseldorf, Tokyo, Singapore and throughout the US).

North-South Travel, Moulsham Mill, Parkway, Chelmsford CM2 7PX ℂ Chelmsford (01245) 492882. All profits are given to projects in the developing world.

Entry regulations Citizens of the UK, Ireland, Austria, Germany, Liechtenstein, Mexico and Switzerland do not require a visa for visits of up to 6 months. Citizens of other countries may be exempt from visa requirements for stays of up to 3 months.

Useful publications *Your Guide to Japan* is an informative booklet containing places of interest, festivals and events and other useful travel data. Available from the Japan National Tourist Organisation, see above; maps, guides, pamphlets and a variety of other tourist literature also available.

Lonely Planet's *Japan - A Travel Survival Kit* £13.95 offers practical, down-to-earth information for budget travellers wanting to explore beyond the usual tourist routes.

Culture Shock! Japan £6.95 introduces the reader to the people, customs, ceremonies, food and culture of Japan, with checklists of dos and don'ts.

Bed & breakfast accommodation

Bed & Breakfast Japan, T273 3-4-12 Natsumi Funabashi-shi, Chiba-Kem, Japan ✆ (81 474) 22 8148 Fax (81 474) 26 0965 offers bed & breakfast accommodation in most major cities of Japan. Cost from ¥4,000 per person per night. Most families are able to speak/understand a little English. Apply 1 month in advance.

A Japanese equivalent to bed & breakfast establishments are the *Minshuku*. These are family-run businesses, the rooms rented out being part of the family's own home. Costs are usually about ¥6,500 per person per night, which includes 2 meals, generally served by the family (¥4,200 without meals if applicable). Details of recommended *Minshuku* are available from the Japanese National Tourist Organisation, see above.

Contacts Another way of getting to know Japan is through the Home Visit System operating in 18 cities, whereby over 900 English-speaking Japanese families voluntarily receive foreign guests. English is spoken by most of the host families and some of the family members also speak French, German and other languages. Those interested should apply in person, at least 24 hours in advance, to the application office in any of the main cities. Further details from the Japan National Tourist Organisation, see above.

KOREA

Korean Embassy 4 Palace Gate, London W8 5NF ✆ 0171-581 0247

Korea National Tourism Corporation 20 George Street, London W1R 9RE ✆ 0171-409 2100 Fax 0171-491 2302

British Embassy 4 Chung-Dong, Chung-Ku, Seoul ✆ (82 2) 735 7341/3

Consulate in Pusan

Electricity 110/220 volts AC

Currency The won (W). Approx W1,240 to £1.

Health Travellers are advised to take precautions against typhoid. Certificates of inoculation against cholera and yellow fever required if travelling through or from an infected area.

Time GMT +9 hours

Travel The following companies can arrange low-cost flights to Korea, and may also be able to help with internal travel, insurance and tours:

Campus Travel, offices throughout the UK, including a student travel centre at 52 Grosvenor Gardens, London SW1W 0AG ✆ 0171-730 8111 or ✆ 0131-668 3303 for Scottish telephone bookings.

Council Travel, 28A Poland Street, London W1V 3DB ✆ 0171-437 7767 (offices also in Paris, Nice, Lyon, Munich, Düsseldorf, Tokyo, Singapore and throughout the US).

North-South Travel, Moulsham Mill, Parkway, Chelmsford CM2 7PX ✆ Chelmsford (01245) 492882. All profits given to projects in the developing world.

STA Travel, 86 Old Brompton Road, London SW7 3LQ/117 Euston Road, London NW1 2SX ✆ 0171-937 9962 (offices also in Birmingham, Bristol, Cambridge, Glasgow, Leeds, Manchester and Oxford).

Entry regulations Visitors with confirmed outbound tickets may stay up to 15 days without visas. Exemption agreements exist with many countries: without a visa UK nationals may stay for up to 90 days; Italian and Portuguese nationals for up to 60 days; most other EU and western European nationals for up to 90 days.

Useful publications Lonely Planet's travel guides *North East Asia on a Shoestring* £9.95

and *Korea - A Travel Survival Kit* £9.95 offer practical, down-to-earth information for budget travellers wanting to explore beyond the usual tourist routes.

Culture Shock! Korea £6 .95 is a guide written for international travellers of any background. The reader is introduced to the people, customs, ceremonies, food and culture of Korea, with checklists of dos and don'ts.

Booklets featuring Korea's historic sites, scenic attractions, recreational facilities, transportation and accommodation are available in English, Japanese and several other languages. Maps also provided. Available from Korea National Tourism Corporation, see above.

Bed & breakfast/Farm accommodation
The closest equivalent to a bed & breakfast establishment is a *minbak*, a system of economical accommodation provided by families who rent one or more of their rooms in their private home to paying guests. Generally, *minbak* were available to Koreans travelling around the country, and some of them are now open to foreign visitors. Prices range from W20,000 per person per night. A booklet listing city and country *minbak* is available from the Korea National Tourism Corporation, see above.

MALAYSIA

Malaysian High Commission 45 Belgrave Square, London SW1X 8OT
✆ 0171-235 8033

Malaysian Tourism Promotion Board
Malaysia House, 57 Trafalgar Square, London WC2N 5DU ✆ 0171-930 7932

British High Commission 185 Jalan Ampang, 50450 Kuala Lumpur, Malaysia
✆ (60 3) 248 2122. Consulates in Johor, Kota Kinabalu, Kuching, Miri and Pinang.

Electricity 220 volts AC

Currency The Malaysian Ringgit (M$), divided into 100 sen. Approx M$4 to £1.

Health Travellers are advised to take precautions against typhoid and malaria. Certificate of inoculation against yellow fever required if travelling from or through an infected area.

Time GMT +8 hours

Travel The following companies can arrange low-cost flights to Malaysia, and may also be able to help with internal travel, insurance and tours:

Campus Travel, offices throughout the UK including a student travel centre at 52 Grosvenor Gardens, London SW1W 0AG ✆ 0171-730 8111 or ✆ 0131-668 3303 for Scottish telephone bookings.

Council Travel, 28A Poland Street, London W1V 3DB ✆ 0171-437 7767 (offices also in Paris, Nice, Lyon, Munich, Düsseldorf, Tokyo, Singapore and throughout the US).

North-South Travel, Moulsham Mill, Parkway, Chelmsford, CM2 7PX ✆ Chelmsford (01245) 492882. All profits are given to projects in the developing world.

STA Travel, 74 Old Brompton Road, London SW7 3LQ ✆ 0171-937 9962 (offices also in Birmingham, Bristol, Cambridge, Glasgow, Leeds, Manchester and Oxford).

Trailfinders Travel Centre, 42-50 Earls Court Road, London W8 6EJ ✆ 0181-938 3366 and Trailfinders, 194 Kensington High Street, London W8 7RG ✆ 0171-938 3939 (also branches in Bristol, Glasgow and Manchester).

Entry regulations UK and Commonwealth citizens (except from India and Sri Lanka) and citizens of Ireland, Switzerland, the Netherlands, San Marino and Liechtenstein do not require a visa. Citizens of other EU countries, Austria, Finland, Iceland, Japan, Norway, South Korea, Sweden Tunisia and the US do not require a visa for visits of up to 3 months; French

nationals wishing to stay longer than
I month must obtain a visa.

Useful publications Lonely Planet's
*Malaysia, Singapore & Brunei - A Travel Survival
Kit* £10.95 and *South East Asia on a Shoestring*
£12.95 offer practical, down-to-earth
information for budget travellers wanting to
explore beyond the usual tourist routes.
Culture Shock! Malaysia £6 .95 is a guide
written for international travellers of any
background. The reader is introduced to the
people, customs, ceremonies, food and
culture of Malaysia, with checklists of dos
and don'ts.

MALTA

Malta High Commission 16 Kensington
Square, London W8 5HH ℅ 0171-938
1712/6

Malta National Tourist Office Mappin
House, Suite 300, 4 Winsley Street, London
WIN 7AR ℅ 0171-323 0506

British High Commission 7 St Anne
Street, Floriana, Malta GC ℅ (356) 233134-7

Currency The Maltese Lira (LM), divided
into 100 cents

Time End September-end March: GMT +1
hour; end March-end September: GMT +2
hours

Travel Campus Travel, 52 Grosvenor
Gardens, London SWIW 0AG ℅ 0171-730
3402 offers student/youth airfares to Malta.

Entry regulations British nationals,
Commonwealth citizens and nationals of the
Council of Europe countries do not require
a visa for stays of up to 3 months. Other
nationals should check visa requirements
with Maltese High Commissions or
Embassies.

Useful publications Information booklets
giving details of Malta's history, climate,
health, accommodation, food, shopping,

places of interest, sport, festivals and other
events are available free from the Malta
National Tourist Organisation, see above.

MEXICO

Mexican Embassy 42 Hertford Street,
London WIY 7TF ℅ 0171-499 8586

Mexican Ministry for Tourism 60-61
Trafalgar Square, London WC2 SDS
℅ 0171-734 1058

British Embassy Lerma 71, Col
Cuauhtémoc, 06500 México City ℅ (52 5)
2072 089
Consulates in Acapulco, Ciudad Juárez,
Guadalajara, Mérida, Monterrey, Tampico,
Tijuana and Veracruz

Electricity I 10 volts AC

Currency The New Peso (NP). Approx
NP5.20 to £I.

Health Travellers are advised to take
precautions against cholera, typhoid and
malaria. Certificate of inoculation against
yellow fever required if travelling from or
through an infected area.

Time GMT -6 to -8 hours

Travel The following companies can
arrange low-cost flights to Mexico, and may
also be able to help with internal travel,
insurance and tours:

Campus Travel, offices throughout the UK,
including 52 Grosvenor Gardens, London
SWIW 0AG ℅ 0171-730 8111 or ℅ 0131-
668 3303 for Scottish telephone bookings.

Council Travel, 28 A Poland Street, London
WIV 3DB ℅ 0171-437 7767 (offices also in
Paris, Nice, Lyon, Munich, Düsseldorf,
Tokyo, Singapore and throughout the US).

North-South Travel, Moulsham Mill, Parkway,
Chelmsford CM2 7PX ℅ Chelmsford

(01245) 492882. All profits given to projects in the developing world.

STA Travel, 86 Old Brompton Road, London SW7 3LQ/117 Euston Road, London NW1 2SX ✆ 0171-937 9962 (offices also in Birmingham, Bristol, Cambridge, Glasgow, Leeds, Manchester and Oxford).

Entry regulations UK, US and most EU nationals must obtain a free Tourist Card which allows entry for stays of up to 3 months. Other nationals should check requirements with the Mexican Consulate.

Useful publications *The Rough Guide to Mexico* £10.99 provides comprehensive background information, with details on getting there, getting around and places to explore.

Lonely Planet's *Mexico - A Travel Survival Kit* £12.95 offers practical, down-to-earth information for budget travellers wanting to explore beyond the usual tourist routes.

NEPAL

Royal Nepalese Embassy 12a Kensington Palace Gardens, London W8 4QU ✆ 0171-229 1594/6231

British Embassy Lainchaur Kathmandu (PO Box 106), Nepal ✆ (977 1) 410583

Electricity 220 volts AC

Currency The Nepalese rupee (NER) divided into 100 paisa

Health Travellers are advised to take precautions against cholera, polio, typhoid and malaria. Certificate of inoculation against yellow fever required if travelling from or through infected area.

Time GMT +5½ hours

Travel The following companies can arrange low-cost flights to Nepal, and may also be able to help with internal travel, insurance and tours:

Campus Travel, offices throughout the UK including a student travel centre at 52 Grosvenor Gardens, London SW1W 0AG ✆ 0171-730 8111 or ✆ 0131-668 3303 for Scottish telephone bookings.

Council Travel, 28 A Poland Street, London W1V 3DB ✆ 0171-437 7767 (offices also in Paris, Nice, Lyon, Munich, Düsseldorf, Tokyo, Singapore and throughout the United States).

North-South Travel, Moulsham Mill, Parkway, Chelmsford CM2 7PX ✆ Chelmsford (01245) 492882. All profits are given to projects in the developing world.

STA Travel, 86 Old Brompton Road, London SW7 3LQ/117 Euston Road, London NW1 2SX ✆ 0171-937 9962 (offices also in Birmingham, Bristol, Cambridge, Glasgow, Leeds, Manchester and Oxford).

Trailfinders Travel Centre, 42-50 Earls Court Road, London W8 6EJ ✆ 0171-938 3366 and Trailfinders, 194 Kensington High Street, London W8 7RG ✆ 0171-938 3939 (also branches in Bristol, Glasgow and Manchester).

Entry regulations Visas are required by all visitors except nationals of India. Tourists can obtain a 7 day visa on arrival, with a 21 day extension available on its expiry.

Useful publications Lonely Planet's *Nepal - A Travel Survival Kit* £8.95, is a handbook for travellers with information on every road-accessible place in Nepal, an introduction to trekking, detailed maps and absorbing background information.

The Rough Guide to Nepal £8.99 provides comprehensive background information, with details on getting there, getting around and places to explore.

NETHERLANDS

Netherlands Embassy 38 Hyde Park Gate, London SW7 5DP ✆ 0171-584 5040

Netherlands Board of Tourism 25-28 Buckingham Gate, London SW1E 6LD Postal address: PO Box 523, London SW1E 6NT ✆ 0891 200 277

British Embassy Lange Voorhout 10, 2514 ED The Hague ✆ (31 70) 364 5800. Consulate in Amsterdam.

British Tourist Authority Stadhouderskade 2 (5e), 1054 ES Amsterdam ✆ (31 20) 685 50 51

Electricity 220 volts AC

Currency The guilder, also known as the florin (Fl), divided into 100 cents. Approx Fl 2.73 to £1.

Time End September-end March: GMT +1 hour; end March end September: GMT +2 hours.

Travel Netherlands Railways, 25/28 Buckingham Gate, London SW1E 6LD ✆ 0171-630 1735 can supply details on the following ticket offers. Bicycle hire available at reduced rates for rail ticket holders at many stations. Rover tickets offer unlimited travel for 7 consecutive days on the Netherlands Railways network; cost from £56. A Public Transport Link Rover, used in conjunction with the Rover, offers unlimited travel on all town and country buses and on the Amsterdam and Rotterdam metro systems. Cost £10 for 7 days. During June-August the Summer Tour Rover allows 2 people unlimited rail travel for 3 days within a 10 day period; cost from £40.50. Summer Tour Rover Plus includes buses, trams and metros; cost from £49.50. The Teenage Rover is available for 4 days within a period of 10 days to those aged 18 and under; cost £24. Teenage Rover Plus includes buses, trams and metros; cost £30. The Benelux Tourrail Card, entitles holders to 5 days unlimited travel, within a specified

period of 1 month on the national railway networks of the Netherlands, Belgium and Luxembourg; cost from £60 (under 26) or from £80 (26+).

Freedom Pass allows 3, 5 or 10 days unlimited travel in 1 month on the railways of the Netherlands. Cost from £24 (under 26) or £31 (26+). Available from Netherlands Railways, see above, or British Rail International Rail Centre, Victoria Station, London SW1V 1JY ✆ 0171-834 2345.

The following companies can arrange low-cost flights to the Netherlands, and may also be able to help with Eurotrain/Inter-Rail passes, internal travel, insurance and tours:

Campus Travel, offices throughout the UK including a student travel centre at 52 Grosvenor Gardens, London SW1W 0AG ✆ 0171-730 3402 or ✆ 0131-668 3303 for Scottish telephone bookings.

Council Travel, 28A Poland Street, London W1V 3DB ✆ 0171-287 3337 (offices also in Paris, Nice, Lyon, Munich, Düsseldorf, Tokyo, Singapore and throughout the US).

Entry regulations EU nationals, and nationals of Canada, do not require visas for stays of up to 3 months. Other nationals should check visa requirements with Netherlands Embassies.

Useful publications The Netherlands Board of Tourism, see above has compiled a brochure listing a selection of books, guides, maps and videos it has to offer.

The Rough Guide to Holland, Belgium and Luxembourg £9.99 and *The Rough Guide to Amsterdam* £7.99 provide comprehensive background information, with details on getting around and places to explore.

Bed & breakfast accommodation Local tourist offices (V V V) throughout the Netherlands can book overnight accommodation in private homes; prices from approx Fl 17.50-Fl 50 per night including breakfast. List available from the Netherlands Board of Tourism, see above.

Bed & Breakfast Holland, Warmondstraat 129 1e, 1058 KV Amsterdam © (31 20) 615 7527 Fax (31 20) 669 1573 can book bed & breakfast accommodation in towns and cities throughout the Netherlands.

NEW ZEALAND

New Zealand High Commission New Zealand House, Haymarket, London SW1Y 4TE © 0891 200288

New Zealand Tourism Board New Zealand House, Haymarket, London SW1Y 4TE © 0171-973 0360

British High Commission 44 Hill Street/ PO Box 1812, Wellington 1, New Zealand © (64 4) 4726 049
Consulates in Auckland and Christchurch

British Tourist Authority Dilworth Building, Corner Queen & Customs Streets, Auckland 1, New Zealand © Auckland (64 9) 3031 446 Fax (64 9) 377 6965

Electricity 230/240 volts, 50 hertz

Currency The New Zealand dollar (NZ$), divided into 100 cents. Approximately NZ$2.60 to £1.

Time End October-mid March: GMT +13 hours; mid March-end October: GMT +12 hours.

Travel Long-Haul Leisurail, PO Box 113, Bretton, Peterborough PE3 8HY © Peterborough (01733) 335599 issue a travelpass providing unlimited travel on trains, buses and ferry. Cost from £133.

The following companies can arrange low-cost flights to New Zealand, and may also be able to help with internal travel, insurance and tours:

Campus Travel, offices throughout the UK including a student travel centre at 52 Grosvenor Gardens, London SW1W 0AG

© 0171-730 8111 or © 0131-668 3303 for Scottish telephone bookings.

Council Travel, 28A Poland Street, London W1V 3DB © 0171-437 7767 (offices also in Paris, Nice, Lyon, Munich, Düsseldorf, Tokyo, Singapore and throughout the US).

North-South Travel, Moulsham Mill, Parkway, Chelmsford CM2 7PX © Chelmsford (01245) 492882. All profits given to projects in the developing world.

STA Travel, 86 Old Brompton Road, London SW7 3LQ/117 Euston Road, London NW1 2SX © 0171-937 9962 (offices also in Birmingham, Bristol, Cambridge, Glasgow, Leeds, Manchester and Oxford).

Entry regulations British citizens do not require a visa for stays of up to 6 months. EU nationals and citizens of some other countries including the United States and Canada may stay for up to 3 months without a visa.

Useful publications A variety of maps and guides are available from New Zealand Tourism Board, see above.

Travellers Survival Kit Australia & New Zealand £9.95, gives information on travelling, local culture, restaurants, beaches and reefs. Published by Vacation Work, 9 Park End Street, Oxford OX1 1HJ © Oxford (01865) 241978.

Lonely Planet's *New Zealand - A Travel Survival Kit* £11.95 offers practical, down-to-earth information for budget travellers wanting to explore beyond the usual tourist routes.

Bed & breakfast/Farm accommodation The New Zealand Tourism Board, see above, publish an annual *Where To Stay Guide* which includes details of independent and chain establishments offering homestay, bed & breakfast and farm accommodation.

The Friendly Kiwi Home Hosting Service, 131A Queen Street, Richmond, Nelson, New Zealand © (64 3) 544 5774 Fax (64 3) 544 5001 arranges home and farmstays throughout the country. Prices from NZ$56.25 per person per day for single bed & breakfast accommodation. Meet and greet service available. H agency will do their best to find suitable accommodation.

Harbour City Homestays, 90 Onslow Road, Wellington, New Zealand ✆ (64 4) 479 3618 provides hospitality with personally selected hosts in and around Wellington. Prices from NZ$50 per person per day for bed and breakfast accommodation. H homes with facilities available.

Hospitality Plus, Connaught Lodge, PO Box 56-175, Auckland 3, New Zealand ✆ (64 9) 810 9175 Fax (64 9) 810 9448 can offer accommodation in over 2,000 homes throughout the country and can also arrange farm visits.

New Zealand Home Hospitality, PO Box 309, Nelson, New Zealand ✆ (64 3) 548 2424 Fax (64 3) 546 9519 provides home hosted accommodation on a go-as-you-please basis with rental car included. Cost from NZ$90 per person per night for shared bed & breakfast.

New Zealand Travel Hosts, 279 Williams Street, Kaiapoi, Christchurch, New Zealand ✆/Fax (64 3) 327 6340 can provide home and farmstay accommodation throughout the country. Prices from NZ$90 for 1 person, full board.

NIGERIA

Nigeria High Commission Nigeria House, 9 Northumberland Avenue, London WC2N 5BX ✆ 0171-839 1244

British High Commission 11 Eleke Crescent, Victoria Island (Private Mail Bag 12136), Nigeria ✆ (234 1) 619531
Visa Section: Chelleram Building, 54 Marina, Lagos ✆ (234 1) 2667061
Deputy High Commissions in Abuja, Ibadan Kaduna and Kano

Electricity 220-240 volts AC

Currency The niala (N), divided into 100 kobo

Health Travellers are advised to take precautions against malaria, cholera, typhoid, polio and yellow fever. Certificate of inoculation against cholera required; also yellow fever if travelling from or through infected area.

Time GMT +1 hour

Travel The following companies can arrange low-cost flights to Nigeria, and may also be able to help with internal travel, insurance and tours:

Campus Travel, offices throughout the UK including a student travel centre at 52 Grosvenor Gardens, London SW1W 0AG ✆ 0171-730 8111 or ✆ 0131-688 3303 for Scottish telephone bookings.

Council Travel, 28A Poland Street, London W1V 3DU ✆ 0171-437 7767 (offices also in Paris, Nice, Lyon, Munich, Düsseldorf, Tokyo, Singapore and throughout the United States).

North-South Travel, Moulsham Mill, Parkway, Chelmsford CM2 7PX ✆ Chelmsford (01245) 492882. All profits given to projects in the developing world.

STA Travel, 86 Old Brompton Road, London SW7 3LQ/117 Euston Road, London NW1 2SX ✆ 0171-937 9962 (offices also in Birmingham, Bristol, Cambridge, Glasgow, Leeds, Manchester and Oxford).

Entry regulations Most nationalities require visas for entry into Nigeria. In Britain the visa costs £30. Other nationalities should check fees and requirements with Nigerian High Commissions or Embassies.

Useful publications Lonely Planet's *West Africa - A Travel Survival Kit* £12.95 offers practical, down-to-earth information for budget travellers wanting to explore beyond the usual tourist routes.

NORWAY

Royal Norwegian Embassy 25 Belgrave Square, London SWIX 8QD © 0171-235 7151

Norwegian National Tourist Office Charles House, 5-11 Lower Regent Street, London SWIY 4LR © 0171-839 6255

British Embassy Thomas Heftyesgate 8, 0264 Oslo 2 © (47) 22 55 2400 Consulates in Alesund, Bergen, Harstad, Haugesund, Kristiansund (N), Kristiansund (S), Stavanger, Tromso and Trondheim

Electricity 220 volts AC

Currency Norwegian Kroner (NKr). Approx NKr10.65 to £1.

Time End September-end March: GMT +1 hour; end March end September: GMT +2 hours

Travel Freedom Pass allows 3, 5 or 10 days unlimited rail travel in 1 month on the railways of Norway. Cost from £68 (under 26) or £89 (26+). Available from British Rail International Rail Centre, Victoria Station, London SWIV IJY © 0171-834 2345

The ScanRail Pass is a flexible rail pass for Scandinavia, valid for unlimited travel during 5 days within 15 days, 10 days within one month and one month consecutive. Cost from £94 (ages under 25) or from £125 (ages 25+) for 5 days. Discounts are offered on certain ferry and bus routes. Details from Norwegian State Railways, 21-24 Cockspur Street, London SWIY 5DA © 0171-930 6666.

Campus Travel can arrange low-cost flights to Norway, and can able to help with Eurotrain/Inter-Rail passes, internal travel, insurance and tours. Offices throughout the UK including a student travel centre at 52 Grosvenor Gardens, London SWIW 0AG © 0171-730 3402 or © 0131-668 3303 for Scottish telephone bookings.

Entry regulations British citizens normally resident in the UK and citizens of other EU countries, Austria, Finland, Iceland and Sweden do not require a visa for stays of up to 3 months. Citizens of other countries should check visa requirements with Norwegian Embassies.

Useful publications Lonely Planet's *Scandinavia and Baltic Europe on a Shoestring* £10.95 offers practical, down-to-earth information for budget travellers wanting to explore beyond the usual tourist routes.

The Rough Guide to Scandinavia £10.99 provides comprehensive background information, with details on getting there, getting around and places to explore.

Michael's Guide to Scandinavia £10.95 is detailed and concise, providing invaluable practical advice for all kinds of travellers. Published by Inbal Travel.

Bed & breakfast/Farm accommodation There is little in the way of bed & breakfast or farm accommodation in Norway; to find out about accommodation in private homes or farms contact the local tourist board in the area you would like to visit. Prices in larger towns range from NKr160, single, to NKr260, double. A list of local tourist boards is available from the Norwegian National Tourist Office, see above.

There are opportunities for young people to stay on a farm in Norway as a working guest. Details are given in *Working Holidays*, the Central Bureau's annual international guide to seasonal job opportunities.

PHILIPPINES

Philippines Embassy 9a Palace Green, London W8 4QE © 0171-937 1600

Philippines Department of Tourism 17 Albemarle Street, London WIX 7HA © 0171-499 5443/5652

British Embassy Floors 15-17 LV Locsin

Building, 6752 Ayala Avenue, Makati, Metro Manila 3116, Philippines ✆ (63 2) 816 7116

Electricity 220 volts AC, 60 cycles (except in Baguio City where it is 110 volts)

Currency The Peso (P), divided into 100 centavos. Approximately P40 to £1.

Health Travellers are advised to take precautions against typhoid and malaria. Certificate of inoculation against cholera, small pox, plague, typhus or yellow fever required if travelling from or through an infected area.

Time GMT + 8 hours

Travel The following companies can arrange low-cost flights to the Philippines, and may also be able to help with internal travel, insurance and tours:

Campus Travel, offices throughout the UK including a student travel centre at 52 Grosvenor Gardens, London SW1W 0AG ✆ 0171-730 8111 or ✆ 0131-668 3303 for Scottish telephone bookings.

North-South Travel, Moulsham Mill, Parkway, Chelmsford CM2 7PX ✆ Chelmsford (01245) 492882. All profits given to projects in the developing world.

STA Travel, 86 Old Brompton Road, London SW7 3LQ/117 Euston Road, London NW1 2SX ✆ 0171-937 9962 (offices also in Birmingham, Bristol, Cambridge, Glasgow, Leeds, Manchester and Oxford).

Entry regulations Except for stateless persons and those from countries with which the Philippines has no diplomatic relations, all visitors may enter without visas and stay for up to 21 days, provided they have a passport valid for at least 1 year and a return ticket or ticket for another destination.

Useful publications Lonely Planet's *Philippines - A Travel Survival Kit* £9.95 and *South East Asia on a Shoestring* £12.95 offer practical, down-to-earth information for budget travellers wanting to explore beyond the usual tourist routes.

Culture Shock! Philippines £6.95, a guide for travellers introducing them to the people, customs, ceremonies, food & culture with a checklist of dos and don'ts.

Contacts The Department of Tourism has a homestay programme in 15 locations outside Manila offering inexpensive accommodation in family homes and an insight into Filipino life; some 295 home-owners are accredited under this programme. Further details from the Tourist Information Center, Gallery Area, Department of Tourism Building, TM Kalaw, Manila, Philippines ✆ (63 2) 59 90 31 ext 146 or (63 2) 50 17 03

There are also homestay associations on the islands of Cebu and Davao; contact the Cebu Homestay Association, c/o Mr Javier Fortunato, Paradise Village, Baniland, Cebu City, Philippines ✆ (63 32) 90786 or Davao Homestay Association, c/o Ligaya Barcinas, 20 Eagle Street, GSIS Matina, Davao City, Philippines.

POLAND

Polish Embassy 47 Portland Place, London WIN 3AG ✆ 0171-580 4324/9 Visa section: Consulate General/73 New Cavendish Street, London WIN 3AG ✆ 0171-580 0476

Polorbis Travel Ltd 82 Mortimer Street, London WIN 7DE ✆ 0171-636 2217

British Embassy Aleje Roz No 1, 00-556 Warsaw, Poland ✆ (48 2) 628 1001-5

Electricity 220 volts AC

Currency The zloty (ZLO), divided into 100 groszy

Time End September-end March: GMT +1 hour; end March-end September: GMT +2 hours

Travel Freedom Pass allows 3, 5, and 10 days unlimited travel in one month on the railways of Poland. Cost from £28 (under 26) or £33 (26+). Available from British Rail International; Rail Centre, Victoria Station, London, W1V 1JY ℂ 0171-834 2345.

Fregata Travel Ltd, 100 Dean Street, London W1V 6AQ ℂ 0171-734 5101 offers express rail travel London - Poznan/Warsaw from £160 return plus couchettes, and a coach service London - Poznan/Warsaw, from £60 return (youth fare). Also flights London - Warsaw /Gdansk/Krakow from £168, and Manchester-Warsaw from £225 plus tax.

Polrailpass entitles the holder to unlimited travel on local and express trains. Valid for 8/15/21/30 days, cost from £35. Available from Polorbis Travel Ltd, see above.

The following companies can arrange low-cost flights to Poland, and may also be able to help with Eurotrain/Inter-Rail passes, internal travel, insurance and tours:

Campus Travel, offices throughout the UK, including a student travel centre at 52 Grosvenor Gardens, London SW1W 0AG ℂ 0171-730 3402 or ℂ 0131-668 3303 for Scottish telephone bookings.

Council Travel, 28A Poland Street, London W1V 3DB ℂ 0171-287 3337 (offices also in Paris, Nice, Lyon, Munich, Düsseldorf, Tokyo, Singapore and throughout the US).

Entry regulations UK nationals holding valid passports may stand in Poland for up to 6 months without a visa. Nationals of most other EU countries and the US do not require a visa for stays of up to 90 days.

Useful publications Lonely Planet's *Poland - A Travel Survival Kit* £10.95 and *Eastern Europe on a Shoestring* £13.95, offer practical information for budget travellers wanting to explore beyond the usual tourist routes.

The Rough Guide to Poland £9.99 provides comprehensive background information, with details on getting there, getting around and places to explore.

PORTUGAL

Portuguese Embassy 11 Belgrave Square, London SW1X 8PP ℂ 0171-235 5331-4
Visa section: Silver City House, 62 Brompton Road, London SW3 1BJ ℂ 0171-581 8722-4

Portuguese National Tourist Office 22/25 Sackville Street, London W1X 1DE ℂ 0171-494 1441

British Embassy 35/37 Rua de S Domingos à Lapa, 1200 Lisbon ℂ (351 1) 396 1191
Consulates in Oporto and Portimao

Electricity 220 volts AC

Currency The Escudo (Es) divided into 100 centavos. Approx Es250 to £1.

Time End September end March: GMT +1 hour; end March-end September: GMT +2 hours

Travel Freedom Pass allows 3, 5 or 10 days travel on the railways of Portugal. Cost from £66 (under 26) or £84 (26+). Available from British Rail International Rail Centre, Victoria Station, London SW1V 1JY ℂ 0171-834 234.

The following companies can arrange low-cost flights to Portugal, and may also be able to help with Eurotrain/Inter-Rail passes, internal travel, insurance and tours:

Campus Travel, offices throughout the UK including 52 Grosvenor Gardens, London SW1W 0AG ℂ 0171-730 3402 or ℂ 0131-668 3303 for Scottish telephone bookings.

Council Travel, 28 A Poland Street, London W1V 3DB ℂ 0171-287 3337 (offices also in Paris, Nice, Lyon, Munich, Düsseldorf, Tokyo, Singapore and throughout the United States).

STA Travel, 86 Old Brompton Road, London SW7 3LQ/117 Euston Road, London NW1 2SX ℂ 0171-937 9921 (offices also in

Birmingham, Bristol, Cambridge, Glasgow, Leeds, Manchester and Oxford).

Entry regulations EU nationals do not require a visa for stays of up to 3 months

Useful publications The Portuguese National Tourist Office see above, publish a brochure providing descriptions of regions, information on food, wines, folklore, handicrafts, fairs, festivals, travel, accommodation and other general information.

The Rough Guide to Portugal £9.99 provides comprehensive background information, with details on getting there, getting around and places to explore.

RUSSIA / FORMER SOVIET UNION

Embassy of the Republic of Armenia
25A Cheniston Gardens, London W8 6TG
✆ 0171-938 5435

Embassy of the Russian Federation
13 Kensington Palace Gardens, London W8 4QX ✆ 0171-229 3628
Consular section: 5 Kensington Palace Gardens, London W8 4QS ✆ 0171-229 8027 *(open 1030-1230; closed Wednesdays)*

British Embassy Sofiiskaya Naberezhnaya 14, Moscow 72 ✆ (7 095) 230 63 33
Consulate in St Petersburg

Embassy of the Republic of Belarus
1 St Stephens Crescent, London W2 5QT
✆ 0171-225 4568

Embassy of Ukraine 78 Kensington Park Road, London W11 2PL ✆ 0171-727 6312
Consular Section: ✆ 0171-243 8923

British Embassy Desyatinna 9, 252025 Kiev, Ukraine ✆ (871 144) 5256 or (7 044) 291 8907

Electricity 220 volts AC

Currency Armenia, Georgia, Kazakhstan, Kyrgyztan, Moldova, Russian Federation, Tajikistan, Turkmenistan and Uzbekistan still use the Rouble, (R), divided into 100 kopeks. In Azerbaijan the unit of currency is the Manat; in Belarus it is the Belarus Rouble; and in Ukraine it is the Karbozamecz

Time GMT +2 to +5 hours.

Travel The following companies can arrange low-cost flights to Russia and the former Soviet Union, and may also be able to help with internal travel, insurance and tours:

Campus Travel, offices throughout the UK including a student travel centre at 52 Grosvenor Gardens, London SW1W 0AG ✆ 0171-730 3402 or ✆ 0131-668 33030 for Scottish telephone bookings.

Council Travel, 28A Poland Street, London W1V 3DB ✆ 0171-437 7767 offices also in Paris, Nice, Lyon, Munich, Düsseldorf, Tokyo, Singapore and throughout the United States).

STA Travel, 86 Old Brompton Road, London SW7 3LQ/117 Euston Road, London NW1 2SX ✆ 0171-937 9921 (offices also in Birmingham, Bristol, Cambridge, Glasgow, Leeds, Manchester and Oxford).

The following companies specialise in travel to central and eastern Europe and the former Soviet Union:

ACO UK, 38 Brooke Road, Princess Risborough, Aylesbury, Buckinghamshire ✆ Aylesbury (01844) 274899

Bob Sopel Ukrainian Travel, 27 Henshaw Street, Oldham OL1 1NH ✆ 0161-633 2232 Fax 0161-633 0825

East-West Travel Ltd, 15 Kensington High Street, London W8 5NP ✆ 0171-938 3211 Fax 0171-938 1077

Fregata Travel Ltd, 100 Dean Street, London W1V 6AQ ✆ 0171-734 5101 Fax 0171-

734 5106. Offices also in Manchester and Nottingham.

FTS Ltd, 49 The Mall, Faversham, Kent ME13 8JN ℂ Faversham (01795) 535718 Fax (01795) 539728

Interchange, Interchange House, 27 Stafford Road, Croydon, Surrey CR0 4NG ℂ 0181-681 3612 Fax 0181-760 0031

Intourist Travel Ltd, Intourist House, 219 Marsh Wall, London E14 9FJ ℂ 0171-538 8600 Fax 0171-538 5967

Key Travel, 94-96 Eversholt Street, London NW1 1BP ℂ 0171-367 4993

One Europe Travel, Research House, Fraser Road, Perivale, Middlesex UB6 7AQ ℂ 0181-566 9424

Page & Moy Ltd, 136-140 London Road, Leicester LE2 1EN ℂ Leicester (0116) 254 2000 Fax (0116) 254 9949

Progressive Tours, 12 Porchester Place, London W2 2BS ℂ 0171-262 1676 Fax 0171-724 6941

Regent Holidays Ltd, 15 John Street, Bristol BS1 2HR ℂ Bristol (0117) 921 1711 Fax (0117) 925 4866

Russia House Ltd, 7 Kingly Court, Kingly Street, London W1R 5LE ℂ 0171-439 1271 Fax 0171-434 0813

Zwemmer Travel Ltd, 28 Denmark Street, London WC2 8HJ ℂ 0171-379 6253

Entry regulations Visas are required for travel to all republics. In Britain, visas for Ukraine, Belarus and Armenia are issued from the relevant embassy in London, while the Russian Consulate handles applications for other states. This situation may change however, so it is worth checking well in advance. An extra charge may be levied for visa application forms submitted less than 2 weeks before the requested visa collection date; and visas will not be issued in less than 24 hours.

Useful publications The Travellers Survival Kit Russia & the Republics £9.95 offers a complete guide for any travellers to Russia and the Republics of Armenia, Azerbaijan, Belarus, Estonia, Georgia, Kazakhstan, Kirkhiziam, Latvia, Lithuania, Moldova, Tajikistan, Turkmenistan, Ukraine and Uzbekhistan. Published by Vacation Work and available from good bookshops.

SINGAPORE

Singapore High Commission 9 Wilton Crescent, London SW1X 8SA ℂ 0171-235 8315

Singapore Tourist Promotion Board First Floor, Carrington House, 126-130 Regent Street, London W1R 7HA ℂ 0171-437 0033

British High Commission Tanglin Road, Singapore 1024 ℂ (65) 473 9333

British Tourist Authority 24 Raffles Place, 20-01 Clifford Centre, Singapore 0104 ℂ (65) 535 2966

Electricity 220-240 volts AC

Currency The Singapore dollar (S$) divided into 100 cents. Approx S$2.35 to £1.

Health Travellers are advised to take precautions against typhoid. Certificate of inoculation against yellow fever required if travelling from or through an infected area.

Time GMT +8 hours

Travel The following companies can arrange low-cost flights to Singapore:

Campus Travel, offices throughout the UK, including a student travel centre at 52 Grosvenor Gardens, London SW1W 0AG ℂ 0171-730 8111 or ℂ 0131-668 3303 for Scottish telephone bookings.

Council Travel, 28 A Poland Street, London W1V 3DB ℂ 0171-937 7767 (offices also in

Paris, Nice, Lyon, Munich, Düsseldorf, Tokyo, Singapore and throughout the US).

North-South Travel, Moulsham Mill, Parkway, Chelmsford CM2 7PX ℭ Chelmsford (01245) 492822. All profits are given to projects in the developing world.

STA Travel, 86 Old Brompton Road, London SW7 3LQ/117 Euston Road, London NW1 2SX ℭ 0171-937 9962 (offices also in Birmingham, Bristol, Cambridge, Glasgow, Leeds, Manchester and Oxford).

Trailfinders Travel Centre, 42-50 Earls Court Road, London W8 6EJ ℭ 0171-938 3366 and Trailfinders, 194 Kensington High Street, London W8 7RG ℭ 0171-938 3939 (also branches in Bristol, Glasgow and Manchester).

Entry regulations Visas are not required for UK and Commonwealth passport holders, US and west European nationals staying up to 3 months. Nationals of most other countries can stay up to 14 days without a visa.

Useful publications Lonely Planet's *Malaysia, Singapore & Brunei - A Travel Survival Kit* £10.95 and *South East Asia on a Shoestring* £12.95 offer practical, down-to-earth information for budget travellers wanting to explore beyond the usual tourist routes.

SOUTH AFRICA

South African High Commission South Africa House, Trafalgar Square, London WC2N 5DP ℭ 0171-930 4488

South African Tourist Board 5-6 Alt Grove, Wimbledon, London SW19 4DZ ℭ 0181-944 8080 Fax 0181-944 6705

British High Commission 255 Hill Street, Pretoria 0002, South Africa ℭ (27 21) 253670-6/7/9 Consulates in Cape Town, Durban, East London, Johannesburg and Port Elizabeth

Electricity 220/230 volts AC

Currency The Rand (R), divided into 100 cents. Approx R5.65 to £1.

Health Travellers are advised to take precautions against malaria, cholera, typhoid and polio. Certificate of inoculation against yellow fever required if travelling from or through an infected area.

Time GMT +2 hours

Travel The following companies can arrange low-cost flights to South Africa, and may also be able to help with internal travel, insurance and tours:

Campus Travel, offices throughout the UK including a student travel centre at 52 Grosvenor Gardens, London SW1W 0AG ℭ 0171-730 2101 or ℭ 0131-668 3303 for Scottish telephone bookings.

Council Travel, 28A Poland Street, London W1V 3DB ℭ 0171-437 7767 (offices also in Paris, Nice, Lyon, Munich, Düsseldorf, Tokyo, Singapore and throughout the US).

North-South Travel, Moulsham Mill, Parkway, Chelmsford CM2 7PX ℭ Chelmsford (01245) 492882. All profits given to projects in the developing world.

STA Travel, 86 Old Brompton Road, London SW7 3LQ/117 Euston Road, London NW1 2SX ℭ 0171-937 9971 (offices also in Birmingham, Bristol, Cambridge, Glasgow, Leeds, Manchester and Oxford).

Entry regulations British and Irish nationals do not require a visa to visit South Africa. Other nationalities should check requirements with diplomatic missions.

Useful publications Lonely Planet's *South Africa, Lesotho & Swaziland - A Travel Survival Kit* £10.95 offers practical, down-to-earth information for budget travellers wanting to explore beyond the usual tourist routes.

Bed & breakfast/Farm accommodation Bed 'N Breakfast South Africa/Stay on a

Farm, Orchard House, Upper Road, Little Cornard, Sudbury, Suffolk CO10 0NZ ✆ (01787) 228494 Fax (01787) 228096 can arrange hospitality in homes and farms throughout South Africa. Prices range from R70 per person per night.

Traveller's Pillow 'N Plate SA, PO Box 27670, 2013 Bertsham, South Africa ✆ (27 11) 680 9040 Fax (27 11) 680 9005 is an organisation of private families offering a bed & breakfast service on a first come, first served basis. List of members can be sent free of charge by mail or fax. Prices range from R70 per person per night.

SPAIN

Spanish Embassy 24 Belgrave Square, London SW1X 8QA ✆ 0171-235 5555/6/7 Visa section: 20 Draycott Place, London SW3 2RZ and 22 Manchester Square, London W1M 5AP ✆ 0171-581 5921

Spanish National Tourist Office 57/58 St James's Street, London SW1A 1LD ✆ 0171-499 0901

British Embassy Calle de Fernando El Santo 16, 28010 Madrid ✆ (34 1) 319 0200 Consulates in Alicante, Barcelona, Bilbao, Ibiza, Lanzarote, Las Palmas, Málaga, Menorca, Palma de Mallorca, Santa Cruz de Tenerife, Santander, Seville, Tarragona and Vigo

British Tourist Authority Torre de Madrid 6/5, Plaza de España 18, 28008 Madrid ✆ (34 1) 541 1396

Electricity 220 volts AC

Currency The peseta (Pta). Approximately Pta200 to £1.

Time End September-end March: GMT +1 hour; end March-end September: GMT +2 hours

Travel Freedom Pass allows 3, 5 or 10 days unlimited travel in 1 month on the railways

of Spain. Cost from £78 (under) 26 or £97 (26+). Available from British Rail International Rail Centre, Victoria Station London SW1V 1JY ✆ 0171-834 2345.

The following companies can arrange low-cost flights to Spain, and may also be able to help with Eurotrain/Inter-Rail passes, internal travel, insurance and tours:

Campus Travel, offices throughout the UK including 52 Grosvenor Gardens, London SW1W 0AG ✆ 0171-730 3402 or ✆ 0131-668 3303 for Scottish telephone bookings.

Council Travel, 28A Poland Street, London W1V 3DB ✆ 0171-937 7767 (offices also in Paris, Nice, Lyon, Munich, Düsseldorf, Tokyo, Singapore and throughout the US).

STA Travel, 86 Old Brompton Road, London SW7 3LQ/117 Euston Road, London NW1 2SX ✆ 0171-937 9921 (offices also in Birmingham, Bristol, Cambridge, Glasgow, Leeds, Manchester and Oxford).

Entry regulations EU nationals and nationals of many other countries do not require a visa for stays of up to 90 days.

Useful publications *The Rough Guide to Spain* £9.99, *The Rough Guide to Andalucia* £8.99 and *The Rough Guide to Barcelona & Catalunya* £8.99 provide comprehensive background information, with details on getting there, getting around and places to explore.

Culture Shock! Spain £6.95 introduces the reader to the people, customs, ceremonies, food and culture of Spain, with checklists of dos and don'ts.

SWEDEN

Swedish Embassy 11 Montagu Place, London W1H 2AL ✆ 0171-724 2101 Consular Section: ✆ 0171-914 6413

Swedish Travel and Tourism Council 73 Welbeck Street, London W1M 8AN

© 0171-935 9784 (open 1000-1300)
© 0891 200280 (24hrs)

British Embassy Skarpögatan 6-8, Box
27819, 11593 Stockholm, Sweden
© (46 8) 667 0140
Consulates in Gothenburg, Luleå, Malmö
and Sundsvell

British Tourist Authority Klarra Norra,
Kyrkogata, 29, 111 22 Stockholm
© (46 8) 21 24 44

Electricity 220 volts AC

Currency Swedish krona (plural: kronor),
divided into 100 ore. Approx SKr12 to £1.

Time End September-end March: GMT +1
hour; end March-end September: GMT +2
hours

Travel Freedom Pass allows 3, 5 or 10 days
unlimited rail travel in one month on the
railways of Sweden. Cost from £68 (under
26) or £92 (26+). Available from British Rail
International Rail Centre, Victoria London
© 0171-834 2345.

The ScanRail Pass is a flexible rail pass for
Scandinavia, valid for unlimited travel during
5 days within 15 days, 10 days within one
month and one month consecutive. Cost
from £94 (ages under 25) or from £125
(ages 25+) for 5 days. Discounts are offered
on certain ferry and bus routes. Details
from Norwegian State Railways, 21-24
Cockspur Street, London SW1Y SDA
© 0171-930 6666.

The following companies can arrange
low-cost flights to Sweden, and may also be
able to help with Eurotrain/Inter-Rail passes,
internal travel, insurance and tours:

Campus Travel, offices throughout the UK
including a student travel centre at 52
Grosvenor Gardens, London SW1W 0AG
© 0171-730 3402 or © 0131-668 3303 for
Scottish telephone bookings.

Council Travel, 28A Poland Street, London
W1V 3DB © 0171-437 3367 (offices also in

Paris, Nice, Lyon, Munich, Düsseldorf,
Tokyo, Singapore and throughout the United
States).

Entry regulations British citizens
normally resident in the UK and citizens of
other EU countries, Austria, Finland, Iceland
and Sweden do not require a visa for stays
of up to 3 months. Citizens of other
countries should check visa requirements
with Swedish embassies.

Useful publications *Sweden Holiday Guide*
is a free magazine providing general
information on travel, places of interest,
public services, medical treatment, eating,
accommodation and outdoor activities, plus
maps and colour photographs. **H** also
Holiday Guide for the Disabled. Available from
the Swedish National Tourist Office, see
above.

Lonely Planet's *Scandinavian and Baltic Europe
on a Shoestring* £10.95 offers practical,
down-to-earth information for budget
travellers wanting to explore beyond the
usual tourist routes.

The Rough Guide to Scandinavia £10.99
provides comprehensive background
information, with details on getting there,
getting around and places to explore.

Michael's Guide to Scandinavia £10.95 is
detailed and concise, providing invaluable
practical advice for all kinds of travellers.
Published by Inbal Travel.

Bed & breakfast/Farm accommodation
A number of Swedish farms offer bed and
breakfast accommodation, with self-catering
facilities available for cooking other meals.
A list can be obtained from Land-Resor,
Vasagatan 12, 105 33 Stockholm © (46 8)
787 5555. Farm holidays are also available
through Holiday Scandinavia Ltd, 28 Hillcrest
Road, Orpington, Kent BR6 9AW
© Orpington (01689) 824958.

SWITZERLAND

Swiss Embassy 16-18 Montagu Place, London W1H 2BQ ✆ 0171-723 0701 Consulate General: Sunley Building, 24th floor, Piccadilly Plaza, Manchester M1 4BT ✆ 0161-236 2933

Swiss National Tourist Office Swiss Centre, Swiss Court, London W1V 8EE ✆ 0171-734 1921

British Embassy Thunstraße 50, 3005 Bern ✆ (41 31) 44 50 21/6 Consulates in Geneva, Lugano, Montreux, Valais and Zurich

British Tourist Authority Limmatquai 78, CH-8001 Zurich ✆ (41 1) 2614277

Electricity 220 volts AC

Currency Swiss Franc (SFr) divided into 100 centimes. Approx SFr2 to £1.

Time End September-end March: GMT +1 hour; end March-end September: GMT +2 hours

Travel Freedom Pass allows 3, 5 or 10 days unlimited travel in 1 month on the railways of Switzerland, including most Swiss private railways. Cost from £66 (under 26) or £86 (26+). Available from British Rail International Rail Centre, Victoria Station, London SW1W 1JY ✆ 0171-834 4325

The Swiss National Tourist Office, see above, issues the Swiss Pass which gives unlimited travel on rail, boat and postbus routes, plus trams and buses in 24 towns, and reductions on mountain railways and cable cars. Valid for 4, 8, 15 or 31 days cost from £91.

The following companies can arrange low-cost flights to Switzerland, and may also be able to help with Eurotrain/Inter-Rail passes, internal travel, insurance and tours:

Campus Travel, offices throughout the UK including a student travel centre at 52

Grosvenor Gardens, London SW1W 0AG ✆ 0171-730 3402 or ✆ 0131-668 3303 for Scottish telephone bookings.

Council Travel, 28A Poland Street, London W1V 3DB ✆ 0171-287 3337 (offices also in Paris, Nice, Lyon, Munich, Düsseldorf, Tokyo, Singapore and throughout the US).

STA Travel, 86 Old Brompton Road, London SW7 3LQ/117 Euston Road, London NW1 2SX ✆ 0171-937 9921 (offices also in Birmingham, Bristol, Cambridge, Glasgow, Leeds, Manchester and Oxford).

Entry regulations Nationals of the UK, EU and EFTA countries, Australia, Brunei, Cyprus, the Czech Republic, Fiji, Finland, Hungary, Israel, Japan, Malaysia, Malta, New Zealand, Poland, Singapore, Slovakia, Slovenia, South Africa, Turkey and all North/Central and South American countries do not require a visa for entry into Switzerland. For further details contact Swiss consulates or embassies.

Useful publications Lonely Planet's *Switzerland - A Travel Survival Kit* £8.95 offers practical, down-to-earth information for budget travellers wanting to explore beyond the usual tourist routes.

Michael's Guide to Switzerland £7.95 is detailed and concise, providing background invaluable practical advice for all kinds of travellers. Published by Inbal Travel and available from good bookshops.

Travel Tips for Switzerland is an information booklet on travel formalities including accommodation, sports and culture. Available from the Swiss National Tourist Office.

Farm accommodation Swiss *Farm Holidays* is an annual brochure with a comprehensive list of farm accommodation; available from the Swiss National Tourist Office, see above.

TAIWAN

Free Chinese Centre Dorland House, Regent Street, London SW1
✆ 071-930 5767

Electricity 110 volts AC

Currency The Taiwan dollar (T$), divided into 100 cents. Approximately T$41 to £1.

Health Certificate of inoculation against cholera and yellow fever required if travelling from or through infected area.

Time GMT +8 hours

Travel The following companies can arrange low-cost flights to Taiwan, and may also be able to help with internal travel, insurance and tours:

Campus Travel, offices throughout the UK including a student travel centre at 52 Grosvenor Gardens, London SW1W 0AG ✆ 0171-730 8111 or ✆ 0131 668 3303 for Scottish telephone bookings.

Council Travel, 28A Poland Street, London W1V 3DB ✆ 0171-437 7767 (offices also in Paris, Nice, Lyon, Munich, Düsseldorf, Tokyo, Singapore and throughout the US).

North-South Travel, Moulsham Mill, Parkway, Chelmsford CM2 7PX ✆ Chelmsford (01245) 492882. All profits go to projects in the developing world.

STA Travel, 86 Old Brompton Road, London SW7 3LQ/117 Euston Road, London NW1 2SX ✆ 0171-937 9962 (offices also in Birmingham, Bristol, Cambridge, Glasgow, Leeds, Manchester and Oxford).

Trailfinders Travel Centre, 42-50 Earls Court Road, London W8 6EJ ✆ 0171-938 3366 and Trailfinders, 194 Kensington High Street, London W8 7RG ✆ 0171-938 3939 (also in Bristol, Glasgow and Manchester).

Entry regulations Visas are required for all nationalities

Useful Publications Lonely Planet's *Taiwan - A Travel Survival Kit* £8.95 offers practical, down-to-earth information for budget travellers wanting to explore beyond the usual tourist routes.

THAILAND

Royal Thai Embassy 29-30 Queen's Gate, London SW7 5JB ✆ 0171-589 0173

Tourism Authority of Thailand 49 Albemarle Street, London W1X 3FE ✆ 0171-499 7679

British Embassy Thanon Witthaya, Bangkok 10330 ✆ (66 2) 253 0191 Consulate in Chiang Mai

Electricity 220 volts AC

Currency The Baht (Bt), divided into 100 satang. Approx Bt38 to £1.

Health Travellers are advised to take precautions against typhoid and malaria

Time GMT +7 hours

Travel The following companies can arrange low-cost flights to Thailand, and may also be able to help with internal travel, insurance and tours:

Campus Travel, offices throughout the UK including a student travel centre at 52 Grosvenor Gardens, London SW1W 0AG ✆ 0171-730 8111 or ✆ 0131-668 3303 for Scottish telephone bookings.

Council Travel, 28A Poland Street, London W1V 3DB ✆ 0171-437 7767 (offices also in Paris, Nice, Lyon, Munich, Düsseldorf, Tokyo, Singapore and throughout the US).

North-South Travel, Moulsham Mill, Parkway, Chelmsford CM2 7PX ✆ Chelmsford (01245) 492882. All profits are given to projects in the developing world.

STA Travel, 86 Old Brompton Road, London

SW7 3LQ/117 Euston Road, London NW1 2SX ℂ 0171-937 9962 (offices also in Birmingham, Bristol, Cambridge, Glasgow, Leeds, Manchester and Oxford).

Trailfinders Travel Centre, 42-50 Earls Court Road, London W8 6EJ ℂ 0181-938 3366 and Trailfinders, 194 Kensington High Street, London W8 7RG ℂ 0171-938 3939 (also branches in Bristol, Glasgow and Manchester).

Entry regulations A passport valid for at least 6 months beyond departure date is required, and visas are required for visits exceeding 15 days

Useful publications Lonely Planet's *Thailand - A Travel Survival Kit* £10.95 and *South East Asia on a Shoestring* £12.95 offer practical, down-to-earth information for budget travellers wanting to explore beyond the usual tourist routes.

The Rough Guide to Thailand £8.99 provides comprehensive background information, with details on getting there, getting around and places to explore.

Culture Shock! Thailand £6.95 introduces the reader to the people, customs, ceremonies, food and culture of Thailand.

TURKEY

Turkish Embassy 43 Belgrave Square, London SW1X 8PA ℂ 0171-235 5252/3/4 Consulate General: Rutland Lodge, Rutland Gardens, London SW7 1BW ℂ 0171-589 0360

Turkish Information Office 1st Floor, 170-173 Piccadilly, London W1V 9DD ℂ 0171-734 8681

British Embassy Sehit Ersan Caddesi 46/A Cankaya, Ankara, Turkey ℂ (90 4) 427 43 10/15

Electricity 220 volts AC

Currency Turkish lira (TL) divided into 100 kurus

Health Travellers are advised to take precautions against cholera, polio, typhoid and malaria

Time End September-end March: GMT +1 hour; end March-end September: GMT +2 hours

Travel Freedom Pass allows 3, 5, or 10 days unlimited travel in 1 month on the railways of Turkey. Cost from £17 (under 26) or £22 (26+). Available from British Rail International Rail Centre, Victoria Station, London W1V 1JY ℂ 0171-834 2345.

The following companies can arrange low-cost flights to Turkey, and may also be able to help with Eurotrain/Inter-Rail passes, internal travel, insurance and tours:

Campus Travel, offices throughout the UK including a student travel centre at 52 Grosvenor Gardens, London SW1W 0AG ℂ 0171-730 3402 or ℂ 0131-668 3303 for Scottish telephone bookings.

Council Travel, 28A Poland Street, London W1V 3DB ℂ 0171-287 3337 (offices also in Paris, Nice, Lyon, Munich, Düsseldorf, Tokyo, Singapore and throughout the United States).

North-South Travel, Moulsham Mill, Parkway, Chelmsford CM2 7PX ℂ Chelmsford (01245) 492882. All profits given to projects in the developing world.

STA Travel, 86 Old Brompton Road, London SW7 3LQ /117 Euston Road, London NW1 2SX ℂ 0171-937 9921 (offices also in Birmingham, Bristol, Cambridge, Glasgow, Leeds, Manchester and Oxford).

Entry regulations UK and Irish nationals require a visa to enter Turkey; these are issued at points of entry and are valid for 3 months, cost £5. Nationals of other EU and most west European countries do not require a visa. Further details available from Turkish consulates or embassies.

Useful publications *Turkey Travel Guide* is a booklet containing information, addresses, accommodation and maps. Available from the Turkish Tourist Office, see above.

Lonely Planet's *Turkey - A Travel Survival Kit* £12.95 offers practical information for budget travellers wanting to explore beyond the usual tourist routes.

The Rough Guide to Turkey £9.99 provides comprehensive background information, with details on getting there, getting around and places to explore.

Michael's Guide to Turkey £7.95 is detailed and concise, providing invaluable practical advice for all kinds of travellers. Published by Inbal travel.

UNITED STATES

US Embassy 24 Grosvenor Square, London W1A 1AE ℗ 0171-499 9000 Visa section: 5 Upper Grosvenor Street, London WIA 21B ℗ 0891 200290

Visit USA Information Service PO Box 1EN, London W1A 1EN ℗ 0171-495 4466

British Embassy 3100 Massachusetts Avenue NW, Washington, DC 20008 ℗ (1 202) 462 1340 Consulates in Anchorage, Atlanta, Boston, Chicago, Cleveland, Dallas, Houston, Kansas City, Los Angeles, Miami, New Orleans, New York, Norfolk, Philadelphia, Portland (OR), St Louis, San Francisco and Seattle

British Tourist Authority 625 N Michigan Avenue, Suite 1510, Chicago, IL 60611 ℗ (1 312) 787 0490 350 South Figueroa Street, Suite 450, Los Angeles, CA 90071 ℗ (1 213) 628 3525 551 Fifth Avenue, New York NY 10176-0799 ℗ (1 212) 986 2200.

Electricity 110/120 volts AC, 60 cycles

Currency The dollar ($), divided into 100 cents. Approximately $1.50 to £1

Time End October-beginning April: GMT -5 to -11 hours; beginning April-end October: GMT -4 to -10 hours

Travel Amtrak's National USA Pass offers unlimited travel on trains; from $219 (15 days). Regional USA Pass offers unlimited travel on trains over key routes in 4 major regions; from $168 (15 days). Bicycle boxes available. Details from Long-Haul Leisurail, PO Box 113, Bretton, Peterborough PE3 8HY ℗ Peterborough (0733) 335599.

Ameripass offers unlimited bus travel, from £50 (4 days). **H** Helping Hand service enables a companion to travel free to assist a handicapped person. Doctor's certificate of eligibility required; wheelchairs and other aids carried free. Tickets must be purchased in Britain. Details from Greyhound International, Sussex House, London Road, East Grinstead RH19 1LD ℗ East Grinstead (0342) 317317 or from Campus Travel, Council Travel or Long-Haul Leisurail.

The following companies can arrange low-cost flights, and may also be able to help with internal travel, insurance and tours:

Campus Travel - offices throughout the UK including a student travel centre at 52 Grosvenor Gardens, London SW1W 0AG ℗ 071-730 8111 or ℗ 031-668 3303 for Scottish telephone bookings.

Council Travel, 28A Poland Street, London W1V 3DB ℗ 071-437 7767 (offices also in Paris, Nice, Lyon, Munich, Düsseldorf, Tokyo, Singapore and throughout the US).

North-South Travel, Moulsham Mill, Parkway, Chelmsford CM2 7PX ℗ Chelmsford (0425) 492882. All profits given to projects in the developing world.

STA Travel, 86 Old Brompton Road, London SW7 3LQ/117 Euston Road, London NW1 2SX ℗ 071-937 9971 (offices also in Birmingham, Bristol, Cambridge, Glasgow, Leeds, Manchester and Oxford).

Entry regulations British and most EU nationals, and nationals of Andorra, Austria,

Brunei, Finland, Iceland, Japan, Liechtenstein, Monaco, New Zealand, Norway, San Marino, Sweden and Switzerland may stay for 90 days without a visa as long as they have an onward or return ticket. Other nationalities should check with US embassies.

Useful publications *Rough Guides* provide comprehensive background information, with details on travelling and places to explore. Titles include *USA* £12.99, *California* £9.99, *Florida* £8.99, *New York* £8.99, *Pacific Northwest* £9.99 and *San Francisco* £8.99.

Culture Shock! USA £6.95 introduces the reader to the customs, food and culture of the United States.

Travellers Survival Kit USA & Canada £9.95, is a down-to-earth guide for travellers. Describes how to cope with the inhabitants, officialdom and way of life. Published by Vacation Work, 9 Park End Street, Oxford OX1 1HJ ✆ Oxford (0865) 241978.

URUGUAY

Uruguay Embassy 2nd Floor, 140 Brompton Road, London SW3 1HY ✆ 0171-584 8192

British Embassy Calle Marco Bruto 1073, 11300 Montevideo, Uruguay ✆ (598 2) 623650

Electricity 220 volts AC

Currency New Uruguayan Peso (NUP), divided into 100 centimos. Approximately NUP3800 to £1.

Health Travellers are advised to take precautions against cholera, typhoid and malaria

Time GMT -3 hours

Travel The following companies can arrange low-cost flights to Uruguay, and may also be able to help with internal travel, insurance and tours:

Campus Travel, offices throughout the UK including a student travel centre at 52 Grosvenor Gardens, London SW1W 0AG ✆ 0171-730 8111 or ✆ 0131-668 3303 for Scottish telephone bookings.

Council Travel, 28A Poland Street, London W1V 3DB ✆ 0171-437 7767 (offices also in Paris, Nice, Lyon, Munich, Düsseldorf, Tokyo, Singapore and throughout the US).

North-South Travel, Moulsham Mill, Parkway, Chelmsford CM2 7PX ✆ Chelmsford (01245) 492882. All profits given to projects in the developing world.

STA Travel, 86 Old Brompton Road, London SW7 3LQ/117 Euston Road, London NW1 2SX ✆ 0171-937 9962 (offices also in Birmingham, Bristol, Cambridge, Glasgow, Leeds, Manchester and Oxford).

Useful publications Lonely Planet's *Argentina, Uruguay & Paraguay - A Travel Survival Kit* £10.95 and *South America on a Shoestring* £16.95 offer practical information for budget travellers wanting to explore beyond the usual tourist routes.

Entry regulations Citizens of Britain and many other countries, including most of western Europe, can enter Uruguay for stays of up to 90 days without a visa

VENEZUELA

Venezuelan Embassy 1 Cromwell Road, London SW7 ✆ 071-584 4206/7 Consular Section: 56 Grafton Way, London W1P 5LB ✆ 071-387 0695

British Embassy Edificio Torre Las Mercedes (Piso 3), Avenida La Estancia, Chuao, Caracas 100, Venezuela ✆ (58 2) 993 4111. Vice-Consulates in Maracaibo, Margarita and Mérida.

Electricity 110 volts AC

Currency The bolivár, divided into 100 céntimos

Health Travellers are advised to take precautions against malaria, typhoid, polio

Time GMT -4 hours

Travel The following companies can arrange low-cost flights to Venezuela, and may also be able to help with internal travel, insurance and tours:

Campus Travel, offices throughout the UK including a student travel centre at 52 Grosvenor Gardens, London SW1W 0AG ✆ 071-730 2101 or ✆ 031-668 3303 for Scottish telephone bookings.

Council Travel, 28A Poland Street, London W1V 3DB & 071-437 7767 (offices also in Paris, Nice, Lyon, Munich, Düsseldorf, Tokyo, Singapore and throughout the US).

North-South Travel, Moulsham Mill, Parkway, Chelmsford CM2 7PX ✆ Chelmsford (0245) 492882. All profits given to projects in the developing world.

STA Travel, 86 Old Brompton Road, London SW7 3LQ/117 Euston Road, London NW1 2SX ✆ 071-937 9971 (offices also in Birmingham, Bristol, Cambridge, Glasgow, Leeds, Manchester and Oxford).

Entry regulations Most nationals require visas. For air travellers a 60-day visa is automatically provided on arrival; those travelling overland may have to pay a fee.

ZIMBABWE

Zimbabwe High Commission
Zimbabwe House, 429 Strand, London WC2R 0SA ✆ 0171-836 7755

British High Commission Stanley House, Jason May Avenue, (PO Box 4490), Harare, Zimbabwe ✆ (263 4) 793781

Electricity 220/230 volts AC

Currency The Zimbabwean dollar (Z$) divided into 100 cents

Health Travellers are advised to take precautions against malaria, cholera, typhoid and polio. Certificates of inoculation against cholera and yellow fever required if travelling from or through an infected area.

Time GMT +2 hours

Travel The following companies can arrange low-cost flights to Zimbabwe, and may also be able to help with internal travel, insurance and tours:

Campus Travel, offices throughout the UK including a student travel centre at 52 Grosvenor Gardens, London SW1W 0AG ✆ 0171-730 2101 or ✆ 0131-668 3303 for Scottish telephone bookings.

Council Travel, 28A Poland Street, London W1V 3DB ✆ 0171-437 7767 (offices also in Paris, Nice, Lyon, Munich, Düsseldorf, Tokyo, Singapore and throughout the US).

North-South Travel, Moulsham Mill, Parkway, Chelmsford CM2 7PX ✆ Chelmsford (01245) 492882. All profits given to projects in the developing world.

STA Travel, 86 Old Brompton Road, London SW7 3LQ/117 Euston Road, London NW1 2SX ✆ 0171-937 9971 (offices also in Birmingham, Bristol, Cambridge, Glasgow, Leeds, Manchester and Oxford).

Entry regulations UK nationals and nationals of most North American and west European countries do not require a visa for stays of up to 6 months

Useful publications Lonely Planet's *Zimbabwe, Botswana & Namibia - A Travel Survival Kit* £10.95 offers practical information for budget travellers wanting to explore beyond the usual tourist routes.

Farm accommodation Farm Holiday Association, PO Box HG 750, Highlands, Zimbabwe ✆ (263 14) 727879/791881 Fax (263 14) 750754 can provide information about holidays on selected farms throughout Zimbabwe.

ORGANISATIONS INDEX

COUNTRIES INDEX

Home From Home is published by the Central
Bureau for Educational Visits & Exchanges, the
UK national office responsible for the provision
of information and advice on all forms of
educational visits and exchanges; the
development and administration of a wide range
of curriculum-related pre-service and in-service
exchange programmes; the linking of educational
establishments and local education authorities
with counterparts abroad; and the organisation
of meetings, workshops and conferences
related to professional international experience.
Its information and advisory services extend
throughout the educational field, and in addition
over 30,000 individual enquiries are answered
each year. Its range of publications cater for
the needs of people of all ages seeking
information on the opportunities available for
educational contacts and travel abroad.

The Central Bureau was established in 1948 by
the British Government and now forms part
of the British Council. It is funded by the
Departments of Education in the United
Kingdom and by the European Union to
promote international education through
exchange and interchange.

Director: Tony Male

Seymour Mews, London W1H 9PE
℡ 0171-486 5101   fax 0171-935 5741

Offices also in Edinburgh ℡ 0131-447 8024
and Belfast ℡ (01232) 664418

REPORT FORM

Up-to-date reports on agencies arranging homestays, exchanges, term stays and home exchanges enable us to improve the accuracy and standard of information in this guide. We would very much appreciate it, therefore, if having completed a stay or exchange you could complete this form and return it to the Information, Print & Design Unit, Central Bureau for Educational Visits & Exchanges, Seymour Mews House, Seymour Mews, London W1H 9PE. **All reports will be treated in strict confidence.**

Name and address of agency/organisation

Homestay, exchange, term stay or home exchange?

Country/countries visited

Length and dates of stay

Age(s) of participant(s)

Was correspondence prompt and satisfactory?

Do you feel you were well matched with partner/family?

Were you satisfied with the financial arrangements?

PLEASE TURN OVER

Were travel arrangements efficient?

Were the accommodation and meals satisfactory?

Were you offered visits/excursions/language tuition?

Were you satisfied with the overall planning of the visit?

Would you recommend this agency/organisation to other people?

Any other comments?

Name

Address

Signed   Date